Children of the Labouring Poor

Children of the Labouring Poor

The working lives of children in nineteenth-century Hertfordshire

Eileen Wallace

Hertfordshire Publications
an imprint of the
University of Hertfordshire Press

First published in Great Britain in 2010 by
Hertfordshire Publications
an imprint of the
University of Hertfordshire Press
College Lane
Hatfield
Hertfordshire
AL10 9AB

British Library Cataloguing in Publication Data
A catalogue record for this book is available from the British Library

ISBN 978-1-905313-49-5

Design by Mathew Lyons
Printed in Great Britain by Hobbs the Printers Ltd

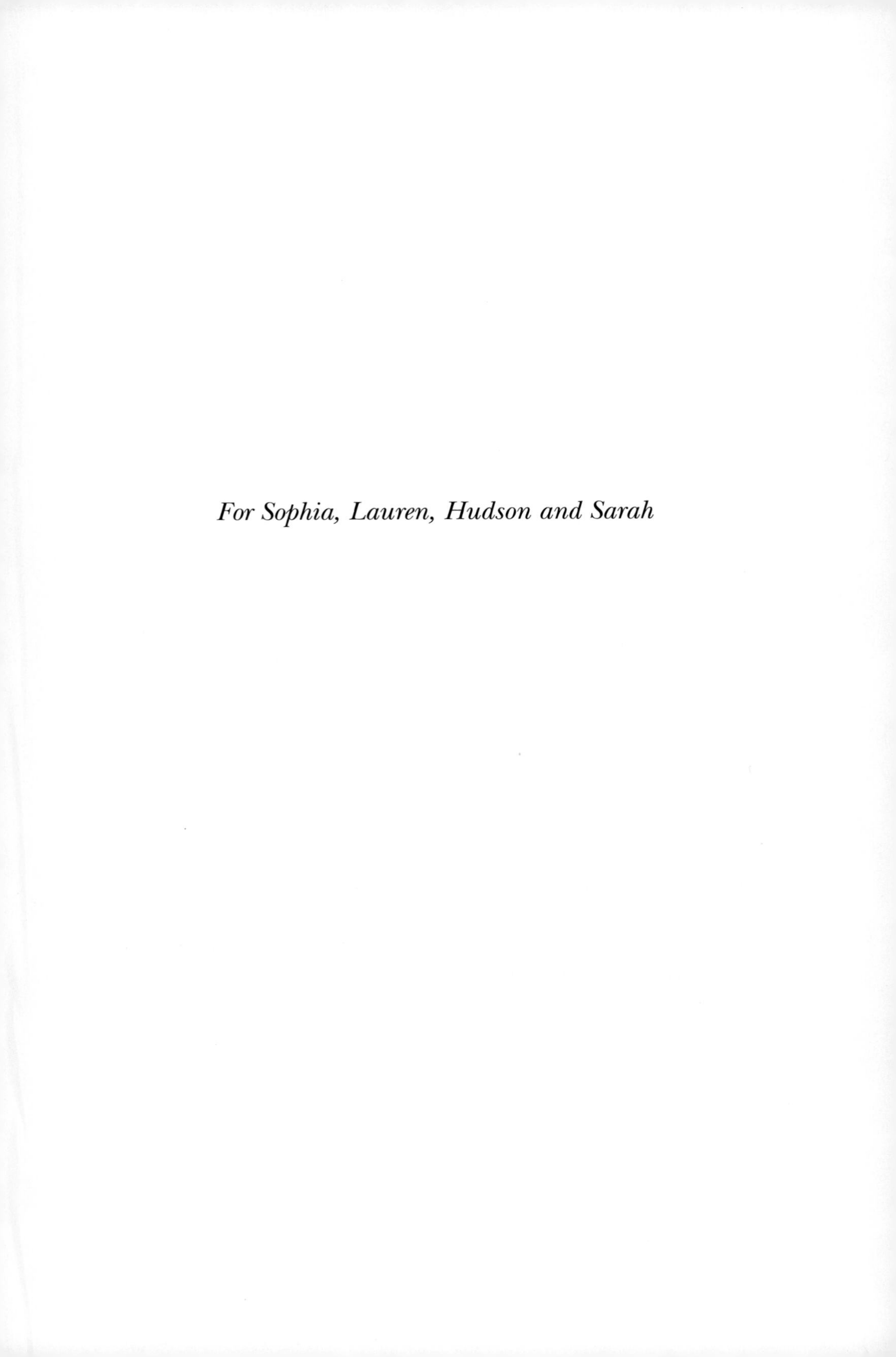

For Sophia, Lauren, Hudson and Sarah

Contents

Illustrations

Acknowledgements

Foremost amongst those whom I thank is Hertfordshire Archives and Local Studies (HALS), the major source for anybody studying the county's history, with its knowledgeable and ever-helpful staff. Judi Thompson collaborated with me in the preparation of a documents pack for schools, which was a precursor to this book, and I am grateful to her. The strength of history societies in most towns and in many villages, with members who research and write with a scholarly approach are a valuable source of information for the local historian. Amongst these I thank in particular Peter Boylan of the Braughing Local History Society, who first drew my attention to the phenomenon of emigration of Hertfordshire paupers from the county to northern cotton mills. Chris Reynolds kindly drew my attention to his work on the St Albans brickfields. Similarly the manuscript diary of Benjamin Woodcock, master of the Barnet Union Workhouse, has long been available at HALS along with the Guardians' Minutes but I am grateful to Gillian Gear for letting me have sight of her introduction to the diary in advance of its publication by the Hertfordshire Record Society, another of the county's historical strengths. I am also grateful to Nigel Goose for allowing me to see one of his relevant unpublished articles. The log books of Potten End School are still at the school and I am very grateful to the headteacher Mrs Senior and her staff for giving me access to them and for being so helpful when I visited. Many other schools have deposited their records at HALS and I am equally grateful to them. My son, Chris Wallace, has been very helpful on the many occasions when the technology of modern writing has baffled me. I thank Bill Neale for letting me have a copy of the Dye family tree and David Shaw for information on the poet Gerald Massey. My thanks are also due to Bridget and David Howlett, who read a draft of some chapters, and to Jim Meacock who read all of the chapters with a fresh eye. Avril Straw helped with the preparation of the manuscript and I thank her. Robert Hodges, Chris Wallace, Alan Fleck, the Bob Grace collection and Sue Flood, the County Archivist, and the staff of Hertford and Hitchin Museums have been very helpful in the selection and preparation of the illustrations and, as appropriate, in giving permission for their use. I would also like to thank Cambridge University Library, the Macclesfield Museum Trust and the Mary Evans Picture Library for permission to use their illustrations. Gary Kirby compiled the index. Finally I acknowledge the tremendous amount of help and support that my husband has given in so many ways. I thank them all but, of course, take responsibility if there are any errors in the book.

The book is about one stratum of children. It is sometimes said that childhood was an invention of the twentieth century, which is, of course, nonsense. In the nineteenth century the distinction between the children of the nobility, gentry and middle class who had a childhood of enjoyment, comfort and learning without manual labour on the one hand, and the majority of children who had none of these things, was stark. As is clear from its title this book is about the latter. During the century great changes took place as a result of work by reformers, some of them aristocrats such as the Earl of Shaftesbury, parliamentarians, inspectors, people with 'bees in their bonnets' such as George Smith, trades unionists and the labouring people themselves insofar as opportunities arose for their views to be heard. Their work had an impact on children, whose lives slowly improved through the century, but it is not the substance of this book; rather it is the background. The reformers have to be acknowledged as sources, since their speeches, writing and actions reveal so much about their times. I have dedicated the book to my four grandchildren, who thankfully have very different lives from those portrayed herein.

Eileen Wallace
Hitchin
December 2009

Abbreviations

BPP	British Parliamentary Papers
CWA	City of Westminster Archives, Westminster
CUL	Cambridge University Library, Cambridge
HALS	Hertfordshire Archives and Local Studies, Hertford
HER M	Hertford Museum, Hertford
HM	Hitchin Museum, Hitchin

Chapter 1

Background to the children's lives

This book examines the lives of children of the labouring poor, those just above or on the edge of poverty, in nineteenth-century Hertfordshire. The living and working conditions of children and young people up to the age of seventeen are examined through documents of the period.

Most children were destined to do some part-time or full-time work from the age of eight in the first half of the century, although by 1900 many children were in school for much of the time. However, children over eleven were legally allowed to work in 1900 under certain conditions. The voices in the documents examined are not usually those of the children or their families but in some of the interviews conducted by factory inspectors the authentic voices of the children themselves can be heard, whatever the agenda behind the questioning. Reminiscences of nineteenth-century childhood in the county, whether seen through a cloud of fond memories or recalled in bitterness, can also throw some light on the lives of these children.

There is an examination of the conditions in which the children lived and the work that they undertook and six of the occupations to be found either all over the county or just in specific areas are scrutinised in more detail. These are agriculture, straw-plaiting, silk-throwing, papermaking, brickmaking and chimney-sweeping. Although some general conclusions can be drawn about children's lives in nineteenth-century Hertfordshire, it is clear that, in Nigel Goose's illuminating phrase, there were 'varieties of childhood' throughout what was a small agricultural county, although increasingly urbanised by the end of the century.[1] Much depended on location, availability of employment of various kinds, family circumstances and access to education. The main variant was the income from the jobs performed by the parents and the degree of their dependence on their children's wages. The experiences of a child in a silk-throwing mill were different from those of a climbing boy and the life of a full-time straw-plaiter was different from that of a child in the brickfields. They all, though, had some things in common; perhaps a rudimentary education, sub-standard housing with little drinkable water, no defence against the ever-present threat of disease, a restricted diet and often inadequate clothing. Their families usually had little or nothing to fall back on if disaster struck such as the death of a parent, a sharp rise in food prices or prolonged unemployment. The possibility of having to apply to the parish for help or, more likely after 1834, of going into the workhouse was always present.

Some Hertfordshire children's lives were often quite different from others due to the effects on different parts of the county of the changes that occurred throughout the nineteenth century. By 1800 the effects of the Industrial Revolution were being felt most in the south-west of the county. The rest of the county remained much more rural. There had always been routes from London mainly through the north-east of Hertfordshire to the north of England. A large amount of agricultural produce was carried along these roads to London and horse manure along with other types of ordure were brought back along the roads and by barge along the Lea to fertilise Hertfordshire's fields. By 1800 the Grand Junction (later Union) Canal stretched from London to Stoke Bruerne in Northamptonshire via Tring. Arthur Young, the noted commentator on agricultural matters, said in 1804 that Hertfordshire was 'generally devoid of manufacture', but by 1800 there were silk mills and paper mills established in the south-west of the county along the banks of the rivers Chess and Gade and by the Grand Junction Canal.[2] In the east of the county the rivers Lea and Stort were being improved for navigation, a process begun in the eighteenth century. The coming of the railways from the 1830s onwards opened up the county still further. The building of railways was a purely speculative venture with no central planning of routes. Each railway company had to raise money, overcome natural obstacles and local opposition and secure an Act of Parliament. The first company to lay down lines in Hertfordshire was the London to Birmingham Railway Company which was encouraged by local businessmen, including David Evans of Tring Mill, to follow the route of the Grand Junction Canal towards Tring. It had reached Boxmoor near Hemel Hempstead by1837 and other lines soon followed. In 1842 a line ran through Bishop's Stortford to Cambridge and by 1850 the Great Northern Railway had reached Hitchin. In 1868 St Albans and the surrounding area were linked to London by rail. Heavy and bulky goods could be moved around more freely and fresh produce such as milk could reach London from Hertfordshire much faster.

Another factor that made an impact was the rise in population that had begun in the eighteenth century and accelerated in the nineteenth century. In 1821 the population of the county was 132,400 and by 1891 had risen to 215,179. One result of this

Figure 1. St Andrews Street, Hitchin. This scene illustrates the high proportion of children in the population, *c*.1890.

was that the number of children under fifteen also increased dramatically. In 1821 there were about 50,000 children under that age living in Hertfordshire; by 1891 there were 77,901. This showed that throughout the century under fifteens comprised well over a third of the total population of the county, even though the death rate was high for children, especially those under five. The large numbers of children in the streets was most noticeable in Hertfordshire towns such as Hertford, Watford and Hitchin. Some of the middle classes responded by forming societies to help the poor, especially poor children. One such society was the Hitchin Society for Bettering the Condition of the Poor, set up in December 1831.[3]

As the century progressed, the standard of living improved for some workers who could take advantage of the cheaper grain from the US and Canada and the refrigerated meat brought from New Zealand and South America. However, the benefits did not often filter down to those on lower incomes such as most agricultural labourers whose wages did not increase but in some cases went down. Mostly this was due to the effects of the depression that hit English agriculture in the last quarter of the nineteenth century due partly to a series of bad harvests in the 1870s combined with competition from imported foodstuffs. The importation of straw plait from the

Far East which helped to bring about the swift decline of the straw plait trade in the 1870s deprived many of the families of agricultural labourers of another source of income (see Chapter 3). Some of the older plaiters carried on with greatly diminished earnings but young workers, mostly girls, had to find other employment such as going into service, into some branch of needlework or into the straw-hat-making trade which continued into the twentieth century.

By the 1890s the silk industry was in decline with only two silk-throwing mills still working at Redbourn and St Albans. The industry did not recover from the effects of Cobden's Treaty of 1860 that allowed French silk goods into England free of duty while English silk goods, when exported, were subject to a duty of up to 30 per cent. Also most paper mills in the county had closed by the 1890s leaving Dickinson's mills at Apsley, Hemel Hempstead and Croxley, Rickmansworth to carry the industry into the twentieth century.

Another aspect to see great changes was education. The setting up of board schools after the 1870 Education Act as well as the move to compulsory schooling in 1880 and free schooling in 1891 meant that the number of working children under eleven dwindled rapidly. The leaving age was raised to twelve in 1901. The transition to full-time schooling unbroken by absence for work or to help in the home did not come easily and it took to the end of the century for most parents to accept that their children could not usually be kept away from school for any reason other than illness.

The thing that did not change much in Hertfordshire during the century was the rigid social structure and the place that the labouring poor occupied in it, for Hertfordshire was a conservative county. Even in church the divisions were emphasised. Many of the better off paid rent for their pews which were then for their exclusive use. The most expensive seats were at the front nearest to the altar, while the poor sat in the free seats at the back or round the sides. To many of the poor this seemed to emphasise their inferior status in a place where they felt all should be treated equally. It would take a devastating world war to begin to make serious cracks in the system.

Childhood and education

When examining the lives of the children brought up in such a society it is important to look at attitudes to childhood. At the beginning of the nineteenth century there were two competing ideas about the nature of childhood and how children should be brought up. The Romantics looked back to the French philosopher Jean Jacques Rousseau's book *Emile* published in 1762. In it he put forward the idea that childhood is the 'one time in life when we can be happy and should be treasured as such'. He also said 'love childhood; indulge in its pleasures, its delightful instincts'. He praised what he saw as the simplicity of country life that would bring great benefits to children. By contrast, there were those within the Church of England and among dissenters, usually called evangelicals, who were very preoccupied with sin and the need for redemption. The *Evangelical* magazine of 1799 urged parents to teach their children that 'they are sinful and polluted creatures'.[4] Some evangelicals like William Wilberforce devoted themselves to opposing the slave trade but others, like Sarah Trimmer, were very interested in the effects of education and tried to stress the importance of bringing up children to lead godly lives so that they could counteract all the depravity within themselves. The inducement could be held out to them that they would reap the rewards in heaven for their lives of toil in this world if they had not succumbed to debauchery and wickedness on the way. It was also important to the evangelicals that poor children should respect the Sabbath and accept their lowly position in life as part of God's order. The idea of children having free time to play, or to be idle as the evangelicals saw it, was anathema to them, as idleness could lead to mischief and later to crime. Many of the middle and upper classes saw the occupation of the children of the lower orders in gainful employment as a blessing in that the children were usually under some sort of supervision and control and therefore not a nuisance to them. Until factory inspectors began to interview them, the labouring poor were not asked what they felt but, although there is little evidence of outright hostility to education, the harsh realities of everyday life meant that the small amounts the children could earn were often vital to family finances. This is illustrated in the following chapters on children's work in different occupations. In a report to Parliament on the *Education of the Lower Orders* in 1818, the committee, which contained some more progressive members of Parliament, concluded that from the returns sent in by the clergy in England, Scotland and Wales 'there is most unquestionable evidence that the anxiety of the poor for education continues not only unabated, but [is] daily increasing, and is to be found equally prevalent in those smaller towns and country districts, where no means of gratifying it are provided by the charitable efforts of the richer classes'.[5] This was probably overstating the case. The lower orders might wish for more education for their children but they also needed their labour and that usually took precedence.

Another report examining education was delivered in 1835 under the less patronising title of *Abstract of answers and returns relative to the state of education in England and Wales*. One witness was the Bishop of London who talked about the superiority of the educated labourer over the uneducated labourer. He was promoting the acquisition of a basic education by the monitorial system used in National and British Schools at the time. This system claimed to provide basic education very cheaply. One master taught older boys called monitors basic lessons that they then taught to groups of younger boys. The bishop advocated the employment of children from the age of eight, especially in agriculture, at the same time as they were being taught to read and write. He did not explain exactly how this was to happen, although he had visited and approved of several plait schools. These were little more than workshops where children were made to produce a set amount of plait and where they might or might not receive some instruction in reading (see Chapter 3). The bishop seemed to approve of the idea of introducing industry into the National schools if possible.[6] His idea seems to have been taken up in Hertfordshire because in 1862 the county's diocesan board of education suggested that plaiting might be allowed more often in parish schools and, if that were not possible, auxiliary schools might be opened to teach plaiting and other subjects.[7]

Rousseau's idea of the idyllic country life was far from that experienced by most working-class Hertfordshire children. Most urban children had some experience of the countryside as it was never far away because of the small size of most of the towns. Agricultural labourers might be their neighbours and sometimes, as in Hitchin, there was a farm near the centre of town. The town children were also used to seeing animals being driven through the streets and livestock markets near the town centres, and some of them may have walked out into the countryside to get away from their slum environments. It is poignant to note that, in evidence given to a Parliamentary Commission in 1832, published in 1833, it was said that, after working twelve hours each day in the silk mill at Watford the children would 'absent themselves from the [Sunday] school and ramble in the fields' instead of attending as they were supposed to do.[8] Rousseau might have approved of their behaviour. In 1839 the children from Aylesbury workhouse who were employed at the Tring silk mill were discovered by a visitor sent by the Board of Guardians, to be playing hockey and other games in a field near the mill on a Sunday. He soon took action to put a stop to that.[9]

There is little evidence, apart from the treatment by fathers, and sometimes mothers, of some young climbing boys and brickmakers, that most parents were cruel or indifferent to their children's sufferings. Many might be concerned about their children's moral welfare as the evangelicals urged them to be, but the realities of surviving in a harsh world, keeping a roof over their heads, having enough money to feed and clothe their children and keeping out of the workhouse was a more immediate concern. From the number of children under eight who were called scholars in the censuses of 1851 and 1861 it seems that working-class parents did try to see that their children had the rudiments of education at Sunday school, dame school or a National or British School, even if the children forgot much of what they had learned when they started work. Large numbers of children attended Sunday schools that often lasted most of the day and taught reading, sometimes writing, and, in a few instances, even ciphering (the four basic rules of arithmetic). There were many arguments about whether and how well poor children should be educated and there was a fear that such children would be educated above their station and disrupt the social structure. In 1840 Leonard Horner, one of the first four factory inspectors to be appointed, reported that he heard the wife of an important church dignitary say that in her opinion 'all the learning which the working classes require is to know the Creed, the Lord's Prayer and the Ten Commandments'.[10] The answers of the clergy to the questions on the provision of education in their parishes in 1818 is illuminating, as much about the clergy themselves as about the state of the schools. A clergyman in Aldbury thought that with only a Sunday school in the parish 'the poor are sufficiently educated for their station in life'. At Kensworth, on the other hand, there were no schools at all and the curate said that 'the poor are without the means of education but desirous of possessing them'.[11]

Most schools, even the Sunday schools, expected the children to attend neatly dressed with hair combed and face and hands clean. For some children this was impossible because they lived in such poverty, either with their parents or on the streets. Many philanthropic people moved by the plight of such children began to provide shelter and some education voluntarily, usually out of their own pockets and by soliciting contributions. Later food and clothing were sometimes provided and trades like shoe-mending were taught. The ragged school movement had begun and in 1844 the Ragged School Union was formed with Lord Shaftesbury, the great reformer, as its president. There were four ragged schools in Hertfordshire in the second half of the nineteenth century, at Hertford, Watford, Hitchin and Barnet. They helped many of the poorest children but they did not long survive the coming of compulsory and free education in 1880 and 1891.

Children's employment

As wages were generally low in Hertfordshire compared with some other counties it was a necessity that most of the children bring in some income to help the family finances from an early age or help at home to release other family members, like the mother, to go out to work. The idea of childhood being a separate stage before adulthood might be taking root among the middle classes but it was a luxury that most working-class families could not afford. The poorer the family the less time there was for any sort of childhood free from responsibilities towards the family. Even in 1890 a Tewin parent could tell the teacher that he was keeping his boy away to help with haymaking because 'the child can earn a little money. We are very poor and sadly need it.'[12]

Figure 2. An errand boy, *c.*1860.

The work done by children obviously varied according to what was available. Hertfordshire was a county of small market towns. Of all the Hertfordshire towns only Watford, from the 1850s onwards, could be classed as an industrial one. There was industrialisation in the south-west with papermaking and silk-throwing, but for the rest of the county there were the trades associated with agriculture like malting and brewing and leatherworking and those that serviced the community. There were plenty of young errand boys and sometimes girls employed by the shopkeepers. In 1851 there were in the county 4 boys of ten and under acting as messengers or errand boys as well as 329 boys and 40 girls between ten and fifteen classed as messengers or porters. In 1861 there were 2 errand boys under ten and the number of those of ten and above had gone down to 164 with no girls in this category. In 1871 there were 5 boys under ten and the number above ten had gone up again to 228. Again no girls were recorded. There is little to show how much they were paid; it must have been a very small amount but it was thought worth having to help their families. Other children appear on the census as baker's boy, butcher's boy or draper's boy. They probably combined running errands with helping with the businesses.[13]

Many children were employed by various tradesmen and craftsmen throughout the county. In 1861 there were 68 boys of ten or under employed by shoemakers and 203 boys and 8 girls aged ten to fifteen. In 1851 40 girls were employed by milliners and 63 were engaged in dressmaking while both sexes were engaged in tailoring.

Children were employed full-time or part-time by plumbers, bricklayers, carpenters, carriers and as grooms and ostlers in inns as well as being inn servants or potboys. Charlotte Langford of Sun Street, Hitchin, a widow and cabinet maker, employed thirteen men and five boys in 1851. Other children worked in plant or watercress nurseries. Lane's

Figure 3. The staff at Hitchin station with ten boys in the front row, c.1900.

Nursery at Potten End employed boys to pull groundsel, pot rhododendrons and tidy up after pruning. For this they received 6d a day.[14] Some children were employed for general duties on railway stations or as telegram boys by the Post Office. Other children who lived near the river Lea or the Grand Junction Canal would help the bargemen and for this they must have needed a certain amount of strength.

Another large group of children who needed strength were those classed as general labourers. In 1851 223 boys were labourers. A poignant case was that of eleven-year-old James Plink who lived with his mother and father in a lodging house in Butcherly Green, a notorious slum area of Hertford. He was entered in the 1851 census as a labourer like his father, but it was noted that his father was blind. There was no occupation given for his mother so he may have been the sole breadwinner.

One substantial source of employment for boys and girls was domestic service. Many of the middle class bemoaned the fact that straw-plaiting practised in certain parts of the county made girls unfit to be servants because they did nothing but plaiting from an early age and did not learn the skills of a housewife, such as cooking, cleaning and sewing. Once the straw plait trade collapsed, however, more children looked for openings in domestic service. Another consideration was that in the case of large families, children would leave their overcrowded cottages for living-in service, allowing a little more room for those left behind. Those in service would usually be fed by their employers, some better than others, and often received cast-off clothing. Some children were employed in the big houses of the county but many more were employed by the middle-class professionals and wealthier tradesmen and shopkeepers. In the 1851 census 346 servants up to the age of fifteen were recorded. In 1861 the number had risen to 553. This included 82 nursemaids under fifteen. In 1871 the number had risen again to 647. Some employers treated their servants well but as there were many families with one servant recorded in the censuses there was always the danger that the servant might be put upon and end up being overworked in an effort to ensure the household ran smoothly. In Berkhamsted in 1851 William Nash, a master bricklayer, employed sixteen-year-old Sarah Richardson as a general servant. In the house were his wife, a dressmaker, her assistant and two apprentices aged fifteen and sixteen plus five children. One hopes that Sarah received some help from other members of the household to cope with ten people's needs. John Ralph, a draper of Berkhamsted, employed a nursemaid of fourteen to look after his eleven-month-old son. This practice of employing quite young girls to look after children was widespread. There were a few instances of ill-treatment and abuse of young servants that came before the courts. A particularly horrific case was reported in the *Hertfordshire Express* on 10 June 1893. Hettie Alderton who came from Broxbourne was sent into service with Mrs Blackmore in Chelmsford. For five weeks all was well, then Mrs Blackmore began to beat the girl and to starve her. Hettie had to sleep on the landing with a rope tied to her wrist but she managed to escape. Mrs Blackmore was put on trial with the neighbours testifying against her and she received a two-year sentence. This is an extreme case but young servants on their own were often at the mercy of their employers.

Wealthier farmers also employed servants. The practice of young, unmarried farm workers living with the farmer had not completely died out in Hertfordshire. The 1851 census records that John Baggett, a widower who farmed 129 acres, had three agricultural labourers living with him, one aged twelve. Robert Smith, a farmer of 460 acres who employed 23 men, had a household consisting of his wife, three children and five servants; one aged sixteen. There was some employment in printing, especially in Watford, and at a type foundry at Two Waters, Hemel Hempstead serviced the industry and employed children. The factory inspector Major Burns visited the foundry in 1843 and recorded interviews with some of the children working there. David Kempster aged thirteen and William Burkake aged sixteen complained of the heat and the fumes, while John Robertson, aged ten, seems to have led a miserable life, being beaten by the man he worked for and by his father who worked at the foundry.

The boys' testimonies were as follows:

Type Foundry, Two Waters, Hemel Hempstead, Hertfordshire. Messrs Wilson and Son

No. 268. *David Kempster* aged 13 years. Examined 23 April 1843

Can't write, can read a little, Attend Mr Longman's Sunday school. Been here above a year. Before [I] worked at the farm. I'd as lieve work here as there. Employed 'breaking off' (when the type is ejected from the mould, a boy has to separate the refuse lead from the type, this is called 'breaking off'). Come to work at 7, leave off at 7 at night, same all year round. One hour each allowed for breakfast and dinner, go home to meals. It is not very hard work, stand to work, feel very tired sometimes, but not so very often, for when I go home to dinner I sit down. Very hot the shop in summer time, makes the sweat run off us. Makes us sick sometimes, and gives us sick headaches; I have been so two or three times, it does not last very long; I was never obliged to stop from work from it, but I warn't very ill; it lasts about 3 days, takes salts for it, it does me good, my father gave it me, he works at the Rost paper mill. Regular pay 5s 4d a fortnight. Hired by Mr Wilson, paid by Mr James Rule; receive my own wages; give them to my father. Plenty of victuals. I hain't been often hit, never been hit to hurt me.

David Kempster his mark

No. 272. *William Burkake* aged 17 years next June. Examined 23 April 1843

Can read a little, can't write. Been here more than 3 years. Employed rubbing types (rubbing them on a stone to smooth them after they have been cast and broken off, the employment of the young boys). Sit at work, it is not over hard but harder than breaking off, or setting up. Very hot in summer, now and then like, not very often, nothing to speak of hardly, a little sick and faint; doesn't last for above three or four hours; goes away and takes a walk when it leaves me. Paid by piece, earn 5s a week. Not allowed to be knocked about. Worked in the fields once, like one as well as the other.

William Burkake his mark

No. 274. *John Robertson* aged 10 years. Examined 23 April 1843

Can read and write. Go to a Sunday school. Been here a twelvemonth. Am a breaker off. Work not very hard, standing or leaning makes my legs ache a little, don't make me sick. Doors and windows open all day in summer time.

> Paid by piece, earns 4s a fortnight. The man we break off for beats me when he thinks I am idle; beats me with a stick, do complain sometimes, was beaten yesterday. My father works here, he sometimes beats me, break off for my father and two more.
>
> (signed) JOHN ROBERTSON[15]

Employment that was very local and seasonal was to be found in Hitchin. For most of the year Hitchin smelled very unpleasant because of its terrible slums and polluted river but for a month or so each summer it smelled pleasantly of lavender that was grown on the slopes around the town. After harvesting the crop, women and children stripped the heads from the stalks, being careful to avoid getting stung by the bees that still lurked among the plants. They worked for either Perks and Llewellyn or William Ransom and Sons. Besides distilling lavender Ransom bought plants and herbs to produce herbal preparations. Women and children in Hitchin and in the villages around collected dandelion roots, poppies, hips, hemlock, belladonna, aconite, buckthorn berries and other plants and herbs to sell to Ransom. Such exertions cannot have earned the children much money because the women who actually harvested the lavender spent long hours binding the stalks into twenty-two pound sheaves for 6d a day and free lemonade. Even so, the pennies earned must have been a welcome addition to the family funds. The sale of lavender was declining at the end of the century because the Victorian preference for lavender over all other scents was being replaced by a vogue for newer more exotic perfumes. The children still had a market for their dandelions and all the other herbs and plants because Ransom and Sons continued to produce herbal products in Hitchin well into the twentieth century.

Housing

Most of the houses and cottages in which the labouring poor and their children lived, be it in town or country, were of very poor quality, with little or no proper water supply, provision of privies, disposal of sewage or enough room to live comfortably. As the population rose, speculative builders filled in every conceivable space among existing houses in town with jerry-built cottages, creating courts with no back entrances and little ventilation. Underfoot was every kind of filth. In an undated article about lavender from the *New Penny Magazine* stuck in a scrapbook, the writer described walking from Hitchin Station into the slum area around Hollow Lane and Dead Street (later renamed Queen Street) and calling it 'so squalid and poor and dismal a town – with beetle-browed buildings and grimy shops and unkempt children and groups of slatternly plaiters'. The writer contrasts this slum area with the rest of Hitchin with its fine open

STRIPPING THE STEMS.

Figure 4. Girls stripping lavender for Perks and Llewellyn of Hitchin.

streets like Bancroft, its comfortable and prosperous businesses, and spacious market square. From the look of the illustrations it was probably written in the 1880s.[16] Another writer likened the Hitchin slums to some of the worst in Whitechapel or the Borough.[17] Such slum areas were not confined to Hitchin. The reports to the Board of Health issued between 1849 and 1853 describe the squalid conditions in Watford, Ware, Hemel Hempstead, Hertford and Hoddesdon.[18] Newspaper reports back up the findings on these towns and highlight the poor state of other towns such as St Albans. In the villages housing was also of a poor standard. Many of the cottages were badly constructed, very small and often damp. Myles Birket Foster, the Victorian artist who went to school in Hitchin, painted picturesque cottages which looked romantic but on closer inspection needed repairs. A book of Birket Foster's engravings was published in 1862. The engravings were accompanied by poems written by Tom Taylor. He first described the scene of a pretty cottage in a flower garden but then went on to describe the reality:

The foul miasma of their crowded rooms

The fever that each autumn deals its dooms
From the rank ditch that stagnates by the door.

The overcrowding, as described in later chapters, was part of most people's lives. In 1874 the Medical Officer of Health for the Buntingford Union reported that in an Anstey cottage two married couples, a grown-up daughter and three children slept in a single room. The son and a lodger slept in a damp cold outhouse.[19] This state of affairs was repeated throughout the county. There were a fortunate few who had enlightened landlords or employers who built adequate housing for their workers but they were very much in the minority. Most landlords showed little concern for improving the homes of their tenants so that many children grew up in appallingly squalid surroundings. In the second half of the century, however, there was a slow improvement as local Boards of Health, Medical Officers, Inspectors of Nuisances and others got to work. The stumbling block was usually money. Ratepayers were keen to have better drainage and water supplies but not so keen to pay for them. Also some landlords such as the Marquess of Salisbury slowed the progress of reform. The Marquess succeeded three times in having any mention of Hertford removed from bills to set up local Boards of Health in towns with high mortality rates when they appeared in the Lords. Many towns and villages had to wait until well into the twentieth century to see a great improvement in the situation.

Health

With such poor housing and a lack of basic amenities health was bound to suffer. Even in 1900 about one in eight children in the county died before their fifth birthday and many more died during childhood of diseases like diphtheria, measles and scarlet fever. William Lucas of Hitchin wrote in his diary on 27 July 1842 that the landlord of the Red Hart in Bucklersbury had lost all his four children in a fortnight to scarlet fever.[20] Every year many people died from tuberculosis or from one of various fevers, the most common being typhus spread by lice and typhoid spread through contaminated drinking water. School log books are full of mention of the effects of illness on attendance. Sometimes the whole school had to close if there was a serious outbreak. It was accepted as a fact of life and in 1864 Mrs Norris, a plait mistress of Berkhamsted, when talking about numbers in her school in 1864 said that 'the fever took off a good many about here a few months ago'.[21]

One of the most feared diseases in the nineteenth century was cholera, which killed about 54,000 people in England during the second outbreak in 1848–9. In Hertford about eighty-one people died, one third of them under twenty. In Hitchin 127 people

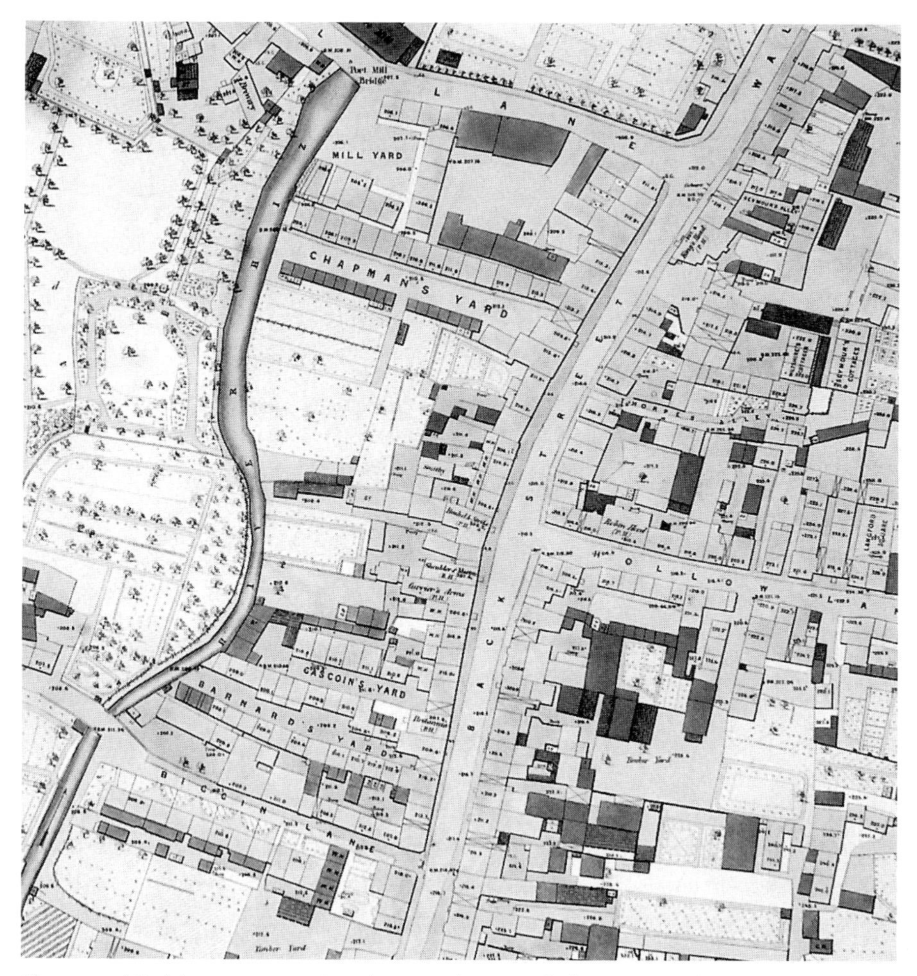

Figure 5. Hitchin town map, 1852, showing the crowded, insanitary slum yards off Dead Street, Hitchin.

died in 1848–9. There was the threat of another outbreak in 1866 and the wealthier people in Hitchin clubbed together to provide diarrhoea mixture free for the poorer inhabitants to try to ward it off. This free medicine was held by every chemist and was on hand at St Andrew's School as well as in the local villages. Hitchin did not suffer from another outbreak in 1866, but whether the medicine had any effect is debatable.[22]

Tuberculosis, which thrives in squalid, ill-ventilated conditions and where people are malnourished, was also greatly feared. People dreaded seeing the first signs of tuberculosis in their friends, usually young people, but there was an acceptance that

Figure 6. Slum housing in Green Street, Butcherley Green, Hertford, which was mentioned in Ranger's report of 1849.

deaths from the disease were very common and a fact of life. In some Hertfordshire towns like Hitchin and Hertford free dispensaries for the poor were founded in the 1820s and 1830s and hospitals were opened in Hertford, Hitchin and Piccott's End in Hemel Hempstead by the 1840s. It was not easy for the poor to gain access to such hospitals because patients had to be recommended by a subscriber to the hospital funds. After 1834 workhouses had some medical facilities but most people relied on neighbours with some practical experience of treating disease.

Diet

Diet was important to the ability of the poor to fight off disease. Those who lived in the county had more chance of getting a healthier diet by growing their own vegetables and gathering such food as nuts and berries from the hedgerows. The meat that most of the poor tasted, if they were able to afford it or to produce their own, was pork. Even in towns many people tried to keep pigs, adding to the squalor. The Hitchin Nuisance Removal Committee, worried by the threat of cholera in 1866, tried to prevent people in the slum areas from keeping pigs among the ramshackle courts. They ordered that ten pigs be removed from Thorpe's Alley and twenty-three from along the Bedford Road.[23] People in towns sometimes kept chickens. In Watford in the 1830s people kept the birds in their cellars at night and let them out to forage among the refuse during the day.[24] The eggs and meat produced were valuable additions to the diet of the poor.

The usual method of cooking was over an open fire as most people could not afford an oven or range. Most food was boiled in a cooking pot. Sometimes there was an oven by the side of the fire or there might be a communal oven such as those which existed at Hopper's Hall in Datchworth and at Harpenden.[25] Twigs, fallen branches and furze (gorse) were burnt on the open fire or used for heating the oven if the occupant had one. Bread was a staple of the diet. If they could be afforded, inferior cuts of meat from the butchers or streaky bacon were used as fillings for dumplings which were widely used to bulk out meals. These dumplings could be taken to work by the men for their lunch. Sometimes they had bloaters (smoked herring) as it was almost impossible to obtain fresh fish any distance from the coast until the coming of the railways. The father in a family, as the main worker and 'breadwinner', usually got the best of the food, the children next and the mother last of all. The opinion was often expressed that many mothers virtually starved themselves rather than let their families go hungry. Milk seems to have been easily obtained, although one doctor spoke of a great deal of milk being sent to London by train, leaving none for the villagers.[26] Often the family might have bread and lard, bread and butter, bread and treacle, or just bread on its own as a meal.

Some housewives in the county were enterprising. One bought the lambs' tails just after the shepherd had docked them and made a lamb stew. A Stevenage mother made rabbit pie from rabbits caught by the Fox twins, notorious poachers. Another extraordinarily fiddly delicacy was sparrow pie. Boys caught sparrows by trapping them in nets held between two poles. In the sixteenth century the vestries that administered parochial affairs declared certain animals and birds such as moles, sparrows, foxes and polecats as vermin which damaged crops and farm animals. People were encouraged to kill them and bring their heads to the vestry officials in exchange for small sums of money. By the nineteenth century the practice had virtually died out but money was still paid for sparrow heads. Some of these sparrows did end up in pies on cottage tables.[27] Such pies were well known and no less a person than Charles Francatelli, chief cook to Queen Victoria, gave a recipe for a pudding made of small birds in his book *A plain cookery book for the working classes* published in 1861. Addressing the 'industrious and intelligent boys who live in the country and are well up in the cunning art of catching small birds' he tells them that when they have caught a couple of dozen they should pluck them, cut off their heads and claws, pick out the gizzards and then hand them to their mothers to boil in the pot with some herbs.[28] Blackbirds were also recommended and this was probably the origin of the nursery rhyme 'Sing a song of sixpence' with its 'four and twenty blackbirds baked in a pie'. Francatelli also suggested that if the mother were lucky enough to have some beef to boil she should give the children the vegetables and dumplings that had been cooked in the same pot and a very small amount of the meat. This would be sufficient for them. Another recipe was entitled 'Thick Milk'. A tablespoon of flour was added to a pint of milk and seasoned with salt. It could be eaten with bread or potato and 'was well adapted for the breakfast of women and children'. Sometimes the poor got a rare treat when landlords, such as the Lawes family at Harpenden, handed out food at Christmas and sold foodstuffs and milk to their tenants at reduced rates. In times of hardship such as the ill-fated cholera year of 1866, which was also a year of cattle plague, the gentry might distribute soup. The log book of Potten End School recorded that children were out of school because they had walked the three miles into Berkhamsted to collect soup from the Hon. Mrs Finch at Berkhamsted Castle in 1866 and 1867.

In 1864 Dr Smith reported to a parliamentary committee on the daily diets of the poor in various counties. He looked at the diet of a family in Harpenden and said that the husband had pork and bread for breakfast and perhaps beer. The rest of the family had tea or milk and bread and butter. For dinner the husband had meat and bread, the family tea, bread and perhaps meat. For supper they all had bread and cheese, sometimes vegetables and occasionally meat.[29]

Later in the century, when the price of imported food had fallen, a Hitchin grocer published in the *Hertfordshire Express* in November 1893 a shopping bill he had found from 1812 and compared it with the prices in 1893.

Commodities	**1812**	**1893**
Tea	10s per lb	1s 10d per lb
Moist sugar	10d per lb	2d per lb
Raisins	10d per lb	5d per lb
Coffee	4s per lb	1s 4d per lb
Candles	1s per lb	4d per lb
Loaf sugar	1s 5d per lb	3d per lb
Yellow soap	9.5d per lb	2.5d per lb

Many people did benefit from cheaper imported food and life must have been a little easier by the end of the century for some of the children of the labouring poor.

Clothing

Most children wore hand-me-downs and boys wore girls' clothing to save money until about the age of five, when they were breeched or put into their first pair of trousers. Boots were the most expensive item and sometimes fathers who were agricultural labourers bought boots for the children out of the extra money they earned at harvest. But boots were often handed down and caused terrible blisters. In school log books there are entries that children could not come to school because they had bad feet. In the straw-plaiting areas girls plaited specifically to buy new clothes or shoes at Easter or Whitsun. Sometimes children had to go without shoes or boots and often clothing was very torn or ragged. It was extremely difficult, especially in the slums in towns, to keep clothes clean or for the children to have a proper wash but many people did try to keep up appearances. One of the punishments used against the pauper apprentice girls in the Tring silk mills was to make them wear 'inferior clothing' on Sundays. Girls who went into service sometimes got their employer's cast-offs and sometimes the gentry distributed clothing and material to the poor. Some of the poor who could spare a little money belonged to clothing clubs and occasionally schools gave back some of the school pence in the form of clothing.

For the girls, keeping their long hair clean was also very difficult and sometimes it was cut off in an effort to stop it becoming lice-ridden. This was a hardship as girls usually wanted to look feminine however poor they were.

Migration in and out of the county

Employers in Hertfordshire recruited pauper children from workhouses in London, and in nearby counties. These children mainly went to the silk mills, especially Tring Mill, but other smaller employers may have recruited them. Mrs Makeham of Fishpool Street, St Albans, is said to have taken six workhouse girls from London, probably eleven or twelve-year-olds, as apprentices in her straw-bonnet-making business in 1830 and 1831.[30] There were children living on barges and helping to work them as they sailed along the Grand Junction Canal. After the Canal Act of 1875 boats were registered and canal children were supposed to go to school where the boat was registered. The Hertfordshire authorities claimed that no boats were registered in the county so they washed their hands of the children. The one time they did take notice was in the 1890s when smallpox was reported on a boat and the inspector chased it all through the locks near Berkhamsted to get the cabin fumigated.

Migration from Hertfordshire to the north

One episode in the 1830s that is not often written about is the attempts of Poor Law Guardians in two Hertfordshire unions to send adults and children to work in the

Figure 7. One of the canal children who travelled along the Grand Junction Canal.

northern factories in the 1830s. This was called 'home migration' and seems to have been the brainchild of Edmund Ashworth who, with his brother Henry, ran cotton mills at Turton near Manchester. After the passing of the 1833 Factory Act the Ashworths and other factory owners said they were desperately short of labour, partly because children under nine years of age could no longer work in the textile factories with the exception of silk mills. The Ashworth brothers were friends of Edwin Chadwick, secretary to the Poor Law Commissioners, and suggested to him that the unemployed labourers in the south and their families should move to the north to work in the mills.

In this way the labourers would be offered a better life and the southern Poor Law Unions would be relieved of having to support them.[31] Letters were sent out to the unions in some of the southern counties including Hertfordshire and two migration agents based in Manchester and Leeds were appointed. Some counties, like Bedfordshire and Essex, took up the offer enthusiastically, seeing it as a way to get rid of idlers and troublemakers. Some of those sent from the two counties settled in the north but many, especially young men, soon came home again causing both the factory owners and the Poor Law Unions to lose money. In Hertfordshire only two unions, Bishop's Stortford and Royston, expressed an interest. In both towns there was fear of rioting after the Swing Riots of 1830 caused by high prices and the introduction of machinery such as the threshing machine that took away the workers' winter employment. There was some arson in the area that made the situation worse. By this time the factory owners were more wary of whom they encouraged to come, saying that 'too many improvident people had been sent' and they stressed that children would be preferred because they were more docile and learned the tasks they had to do more easily. Manual dexterity was needed and children's hands were not yet hardened by agricultural labour.

Bishop's Stortford supplied a list of thirty-seven children thought suitable. William and Ralph Turner, Lancashire cotton mill owners, agreed to take eleven girls as apprentices provided that a man and his wife who was to act as matron were sent with them and the children were to be decently clothed with a Sunday change of clothes. The girls would be taken by wagon to London and then on board one of Mr Pickford's barges to take them to Lancashire, a journey of four days. The guardians had also to contribute to the furnishing of the cottage in which the children would live. The girls would be bound apprentice until the age of twenty and would be paid from 2s 6d to 4s. 6d at first, rising to between 5s 6d and 6s 6d when they reached twenty.[32]

In the case of Royston the clerk to the union, Mr Thurall, was very enthusiastic about the project but was disappointed that orphan girls seemed to be preferred to young men. He wrote of his own volition to a pottery manufacturer in Burslem offering unemployed single males from Royston work in Staffordshire. No reply is recorded. Thurall tried to arrange for twelve to fourteen orphan children to go to Ashworth's mill at Turton. He enquired of Pickfords whether their boats went to Turton. There is no evidence that the children were ever sent. At least three families did go north from Royston because one father named Racher came back from Turton to ask the Royston Union for help as his wife and daughter were ill and could not work. It is not clear whether the families stayed or what happened to the children from Bishop's Stortford. The project had been dropped by the late 1830s when there was a slump in the cotton trade.[33] There was also some emigration to the United States, Canada and Australia, aided by the Poor Law Unions. Six adults and nine children left Royston for Quebec and a family with two children from Barley in the Royston Union also left for Canada in 1836.[34]

Involvement with the law

Some Hertfordshire children did not have any choice about emigrating. During the course of the century 39 children under sixteen, including one girl, were transported to Australia. Many were sentenced for what today we would regard as petty crimes but some were charged with more serious offences such as highway robbery and attempted murder. Between 1800 and 1852 fifty-seven children aged between nine and fifteen were brought before the courts on charges that, if they were found guilty, would incur sentences ranging from seven years to life imprisonment. Nine were sentenced to death for stealing sheep or horses, arson or highway robbery. The most serious charge was against Jane Kitson aged thirteen who was found guilty of attempting to murder George Alsbury in 1813 and was sentenced to death. Thomas Chalkley, an eleven-year-old from Stevenage, was also sentenced to death for stealing £16 in 1827. Luckily for both of them their death sentences were commuted to transportation for life. Eleven children were sentenced to imprisonment in Parkhurst on the Isle of Wight which was opened in 1838 as a prison for juvenile offenders.[35] Punishments were also harsh in the lesser courts. Thomas Grey aged eleven of North Mymms stole a sovereign in 1840 and was transported for seven years. Frederick Edwards aged fifteen stole two cigars worth 4d in 1847 and was also given seven years' transportation.[36] At the juvenile sessions that dealt with children under fourteen, harsh, if shorter, sentences were handed down for minor crimes. In 1863 James Law was found guilty of stealing one jacket. He was sentenced to one calendar month in gaol and four years in a reform school. In the same year Elizabeth Judd was sentenced to two days' hard labour for stealing a straw hat. A number were also privately whipped. In 1875 the *Hertfordshire Mercury* reported the case of David Warner who stole two apples. He was fined 1s 6d plus 8s costs with one week's imprisonment in default. He probably went to prison because his family could ill afford to lose nearly a week's wages.[37] Employers who broke the law and whose actions or neglect sometimes caused deaths were merely fined and cautioned.

Diversions and amusements

Times were hard for many of the children of the labouring poor but they seized every opportunity to make their lives a little brighter. If they had full-time jobs they usually had a day off at Christmas, Easter and Whitsun until the coming of bank holidays in 1871 when they had a little more free time. School log books were diaries kept by headteachers detailing the day-to-day running of schools including attendance. They show the effects of outside attractions, great and small, on the attendance of pupils. The extracts from the log book of St Mary's Boys' School, Hitchin, at the end of this chapter illustrate the interruptions to school life. One such event was the market usually held weekly in most Hertfordshire towns. The bustle of the market could be exciting to children and many were pleased when their mothers let them accompany them to the plait market or to the ordinary market to buy provisions which meant missing school. Sunday school treats were another highlight. The treat might be only marching to a field with banners and flags to play games and have a tea of bread and butter and cake, but it was eagerly anticipated. Some children were adept at attending as many Sunday school treats as possible, whether they had any connection with the church or not. School treats were also popular with games and races, and in the villages the local gentry might allow the school to use their grounds as Mrs Finch did each year at Berkhamsted Castle for Potten End School in the 1860s.

Fairs came yearly to many towns and caused great excitement. Sometimes, as at Berkhamsted, they were held on Whit Monday when most of the children in the silk mills and paper mills had the day off. These had often been hiring fairs but by the second half of the nineteenth century most were purely amusement fairs and children saved their pennies for months to pay for rides. Sometimes a travelling theatrical company came at the same time as the fair as happened at Harpenden in the 1860s and 1870s. Occasionally a circus would visit and cause great excitement when it paraded through the town. Most schools bowed to the inevitable and closed for the half-day when this happened. May Day was celebrated in towns and villages and was traditionally associated with sweeps who were supposed to bring good luck although no one could say why. Sweeps and mummers paraded around various towns in which sweep families lived such as Ware, Hertford, Hitchin and Tring. They danced and sang traditional songs while soliciting pennies from householders. In the villages the harvest home ceremony, when the final sheathes were ceremonially brought back to the barn and a harvest supper was held with the farmers footing the bill, was the highlight of the year. Another annual event that was eagerly awaited was 5 November, bonfire night. Most towns and villages had bonfires and some could even afford fireworks.

Sometimes there were unexpected events as happened in 1837 when a balloon that had started its flight at Vauxhall Gardens in London landed in a field in Offley causing great excitement.[38] The opening of Digswell viaduct and the various railway stations must have been occasions to remember. The navvies who built the railways had caused a great stir and their bare-knuckle fights were legendary.[39] There were also more gentle

Figure 8. The annual May Day dance in Hitchin.

gatherings. Benevolent employers sometimes gave their workers a dinner. In the 1840s Phebe Lucas wrote about the New Year's supper her father, a brewer and maltster, gave for his employees in Hitchin. The men ate in the kitchen but the boys had tables in the washhouse. They all feasted on roast or boiled beef and mutton and plum pudding.[40]

In many places in Hertfordshire royal visits and special occasions were celebrated and the towns and villages were decked out with flags and festive arches appropriate to the locality. One such decoration was made of straw plait. Queen Victoria's coronation was the reason for a spectacular celebration in Hitchin. On 28 June 1837 the shops were shut for the day and it is said that 1,300 people including children over twelve dined on beef and plum puddings. The younger children were given plum buns as a consolation for not being allowed to sit down at the meal. It must have been a memorable sight.[41]

St Mary's School, Hitchin: Extract from log book[42]

School log books give a clear understanding of the various reasons why children did not attend school. Some of these were related to work, such as farm work, plaiting, brickmaking and other employment, or other events.

These selected examples (covering 1863–6) from St Mary's School, a National School for boys at Hitchin, illustrate the various problems faced by the schoolmaster, although he seems to have declared half-day holidays for the slightest reason and often closed an afternoon session if the attendance was too low. There are also glimpses of attractions and 'treats' for the children.

1863

22 January	Holiday in afternoon for treat.
9 July	Holiday in afternoon for Sunday school treat.
31 July	School greatly fallen off in consequence of harvest.
3–7 August	Very small attendance for harvest. Average rarely exceeding 30. School broke up.
14 September	School re-opens after five weeks holiday with a fair number of scholars as usual.
22 September	Small school. Holiday in the afternoon.
24 September	Small school in consequence of Agricultural Show. Holiday in afternoon.
18 December	School broke up for the Christmas holidays. Fortnight allowed.

1864

4 January	Holiday in the afternoon.
28 April	The examination continued by the inspector. Boys had holiday in the afternoon.
31 May	Closed school early this afternoon in order to allow the boys to go to an entertainment in the town hall.
13 June	Rev. Hemsley (Chair of the Board) brought in the results from the Government of the examination and the Schedule for grant showing that of the school's 55 enrolled pupils the average present for the examinations was 39. As a result the school's grant was £18 16s 9d [the grant was determined by a combination of attendance and attainment in tests; poor attendance affected both].

29 June	School as usual except very full. In morning 64, in afternoon 68 present.
12 July	Small school this morning. Holiday in afternoon for Sunday school treat.
20 July	Several boys punished for being late.
25 July	The school seems to be falling off in numbers. Many boys absent at field work.
1 August	Find the school greatly falling off owing to the harvest.
5 August	School broke up for Harvest holidays.
5 September	School re-opened after holidays. Rather thin attendance.
12 September	The school slightly improved in numbers.
13 September	Punished several boys for being late.
3 October	School greatly improved in numbers. Night school opened.
10 October	Numbers steadily increase.
20 October	Punished several boys for coming late. Still find great trouble from this fault.
24 October	No boys late today.
25 October	Thin school owing to market.
3 November	Two boys punished for playing truant.
15 November	Thin school. Much fever about.
18 November	The school seems to be getting thinner. The fever will account for it.
1 December	Fever in master's house. Master forced to keep out of school.
12 December	Master returned.
13 December	School seems to have fallen off in the meantime.

1865

9 January	School re-opened after the Christmas holidays. Numbers very fair.
20 January	No boys late today.
14 February	Thin school owing to market.
29 March	Called the attention of the pupil teacher to his method of delivering a lesson. Wants a more cheerful tone.

24 April	School re-opened after two weeks' [Easter] break.
26 April	Mr Robinson the Inspector examined the school in the afternoon. Numbers presented 48.
27 April	Boys had holiday in the afternoon, the examination being finished.
25 May	Holiday on account of Ascension Day.
2 June	School broke up for a week's holiday. Whitsun week.
12 June	School re-assembles after week's holiday. Numbers fair.
16 June	Master absent for two months from lameness and general disability. Not able to be in school.
19 July	Summary of inspector's report; attainments respectable but 'not good enough for such an important parish', not enough boys reaching standard 3. Result is that the school's grant was reduced by one tenth.
4 September	School re-opens after the Harvest Vacation. Gleaning not being over, attendance is very thin, 33 and 36 being the numbers.
24 September	Attendance very thin indeed in afternoon. Several boys gone to their choirmaster's for tea.
27 September	Boys had half-holiday in afternoon, school got ready for luncheon on Thursday.
28 September	A holiday in consequence of the luncheon given to subscribers to the restoration fund [for the church].
26 October	Another wet day; attendance very thin.
31 October	Market day. Attendance down. School very cold and uncomfortable.
6 November	Anniversary of the Gunpowder Treason commemorated today. Attendance very thin. [5 November fell on a Sunday that year so the bonfire was lit on Monday]
9 November	I [The master] did not go into school today as I am assisting in the bazaar preparation. In afternoon there was a holiday as the Bazaar held in the Girls' and Infants' Schools was in aid of our school.

10 November Another half day holiday for same reason as above. In the morning [took] about 11 boys through the other schools to see the Bazaar. They were pleased. Two [pupil] teachers managed the evening school as I was out of town. Attendance very thin.

13 November Frank [who had been a pupil-teacher at the school before winning a first-class scholarship to attend St Mark's College, the National Schools' training college, where he had passed to be an assistant teacher at St Mary's] in charge of the school today as I was away. Attendance good in day and night school.

30 November St Andrew's Day. Took the school to church at 11am.

1 December A large incendiary fire close to the school broke out at about 1.20am. No school until the building was out of danger. All day a crowd of adults and boys have been in playground and have been a great inconvenience. The smell of burnt wood is very disagreeable. Attendance very thin in the afternoon. After 2.15 left Frank in charge as I had to meet a friend at the station. Attendance at night school very low.

14 December Still very cold in school. Dismissed at 4 in the afternoon and 1.15 in the morning.

15 December Scripture exam. 34 boys were present instead of 102 possible. The attendance is very thin.

19 December A 'Giant and Dwarf' show attracted many night scholars. There were so few in attendance that the class was dismissed.

20 December I was so busy indoors that I left Frank in charge in the afternoon.

21 December St Thomas's Day. I was away. Frank took the school to church at 11am. and was in charge all day.

22 December Frank dismissed the school at 12.15 for the Christmas holidays.

1866

15 January There was a good attendance of the night school for the first night after the holiday and all the lads worked well.

16 January	Market Day and a very wet one, Attendance miserably thin. Only 10 boys in the afternoon first and second classes.
24 January	Night school full.
25 January	Conversion of St Paul. Took the boys to church in the morning.
29 January	Attendance very large. Several new boys. In the morning I went to several of the gentry to ask for a few evergreens [to decorate school]. Frank and some of the boys went to fetch them.
31 January	No night school in consequence of the choir's concert.
1 February	Boys assemble in the morning and after a little singing, we gave them their treat tickets. No afternoon school.
2 February	The annual Treat of the school was held today. 74 boys out of 75 were present. Tea was followed by singing, a Christmas tree and magic lantern. From the tree prizes were given for the children who had attended most regularly since Easter. Five boys received very handsome pictures. No night school.
7 February	Attendance in day school much better. Still very thin in evening. Such a large proportion came late so for the future I intend caning the culprits as well as keeping them in after school.
8 February	Not nearly so many late in the morning and only two in the afternoon.
14 February	Ash Wednesday. Boys to church at 11am instead of scripture.
19 February	Today I began using absentee papers upon which the absentee will bring the reason for their absence.
20 February	Market day thinned attendance a little. Mr Pardoe helped in evening school. I left at 7.30.
22 February	Thin attendance in morning because of the cold.
27 February	Snow was deep today and attendance low.
8 March	After school in the morning a Professor of Magic came to entertain the boys.

9 March	Today was one of Humiliation [to pray for the cattle plague to be lifted] appointed by the Bishop of the Diocese. Boys attended 10am and registers marked at 10.30. Thin attendance. Went to church at 11. In the afternoon only 19 boys came and dismissed them. No evening class.
14 March	In the evening the scholars 29 in all who had made up their 24 attendances had supper in the school. They met at 7 and had several games and at 8 supper. All were delighted with the evening.
21 March	Snow and rain; attendance very low. School very cold.
29 March	Attendance thin this morning. At 3pm I dismissed the boys for the Easter Vac.
7 April	I visited parents of candidates absent from exam. All promised to send them in.
9 April	Market day. Several boys at work in the fields.
11 April	Attendance much better.
16 April	A circus kept more than half the boys away. 26 asked for leave. The attendance was so thin I did not call the register.
19 April	I punished severely the 10 boys who stayed away from school the previous afternoon without leave.
27 April	Attendance very good for a Friday. In afternoon I called register at 2 and dismissed at 4 as the woman wanted to begin scouring the floor and desks.
1 May	St Philip and St James Day. Went to church at 11am.
1 June	Attendance still very fluctuating. The highest was only 74. Every dinner-hour this week Frank and I have played at cricket with the boys.
15 June	Attendance thin, cause unknown.
22 June	Several boys away hay-making.
25 June	Attendance very high.
27 June	Went with boys to Crystal Palace. Left Frank in charge. Attendance very low in afternoon. Several boys went to see a cricket match.

29 June	St Peter's Day. Registration at 9.30. Omitted scripture lesson. School to church at 11.30am. Punished several boys after for misconduct.
2 July	Attendance excellent today.
10 July	Market day. Attendance low all day, almost 20 fewer than previous day.
11 July	In the afternoon gave school half-holiday as I promised boys one if 80 boys attended at once. Wesleyan Sunday school treat kept several boys [away] in the morning.
12 July	Attendance low in afternoon with 79 present. The heat was intense.
20 July	School in afternoon very low. On Saturday the boys played the British School at cricket and lost by only 4 runs.
25 July	St James's Day. 3 boys came before registration, 2 after registration at 9.30. At 11.30 we took the whole school to church [that means the 5 boys and however many girls and infants who turned up for school]
27 July	Only 8 boys present in the first class.
1 August	Frank in afternoon took twelve boys to cricket. Attendance good all day. Drilled the boys half-an-hour in afternoon.
3 August	Vacation after giving them circulars informing parents how long the vacations lasted.

Endnotes

1. N. Goose, 'Child employment prospects in nineteenth-century Hertfordshire in perspective: varieties of childhood?', unpublished article.
2. A. Young, *General view of the agriculture of Hertfordshire* (originally published 1804, reprinted Newton Abbot, 1971), p. 221.
3. Lawson Thompson scrapbook, Hitchin Museum (hereafter HM), vol. 1B, p. 155.
4. H. Cunningham, *The invention of childhood* (London, 2006), p. 130.
5. British Parliamentary Papers (hereafter BPP) 1818 (136) IV.1, *Report from the select committee on the education of the lower orders.*
6. BPP 1835 (62) XLI.1–XLIII.1, *Abstract of answers and returns relative to the state of education in England and Wales.*
7. J.G. Dony, *A history of the straw hat industry* (Luton, 1942), p. 80.

8. BPP 1833 (450) XX.1, *Royal commission on the employment of children in factories.*
9. Aylesbury board of guardians minute book, 1838–9, Centre for Buckinghamshire Studies, Aylesbury, G/2/3.
10. L. Horner, *On the employment of children: in factories and other works in the United Kingdom and in some foreign countries* (London, 1840), p. 17.
11. BPP 1818 (136) IV.1, *Report from the select committee on the education of the lower orders.*
12. Quoted in S. James (ed.), *Two hundred years of Tewin School* (Tewin, 1992), p. 19.
13. BPP, statistical tables issued after each census which include figures for occupations broken down by age, 1841–91, Hertfordshire Archives and Local Studies (hereafter HALS).
14. V.J.M. Bryant, *A history of Potten End* (Cheshunt, 1986), p. 50.
15. BPP 1843 (431) XIV.1, *Children's employment commission*, pp. 46–7.
16. Lawson Thompson scrapbook, HM, vol. 1A, p. 53.
17. J. Brown, *The English market town* (Marlborough, 1986), p. 133.
18. *Reports to the general board of health* issued for the following towns in Hertfordshire: Great Amwell and Ware, Hertford, Hitchin, Hoddesdon, Hemel Hempstead and Watford, HALS.
19. Buntingford rural sanitary committee papers, 1872–8, HALS RDC4/4G/112.
20. G. Bryant and G. Baker (eds), *W. Lucas, a Quaker Journal*, 1804–61, two volumes (London, 1934), vol. 2, p. 22.
21. BBP 1864 (3414) XXII.1, *Children's employment commission* (1862), evidence to Mr J. E. White.
22. Hitchin nuisance removal committee minutes, July–November, 1866, p. 13, HALS BG/HIT/276.
23. *Ibid.*
24. J. Coutts Smith (compiler), *A Hertfordshire sampler* (Hertford, 1980), p. 96.
25. T.O. Beachcroft and W.B. Emms, *Five hide village: a history of Datchworth in Hertfordshire* (Datchworth, 1984); E. Grey, *Cottage life in a Hertfordshire village: How the Agricultural Labourers lived and fared in the late 1860s and 70s* (St Albans, 1934, reprinted Harpenden, 1977), p. 96.
26. BPP 1867–8 (4068) XVII.1, *Commission on the employment of children, young persons and women in agriculture* (1867).
27. Coutts Smith, *A Hertfordshire sampler*, p. 119.
28. C.E.M. Francatelli, *A plain cookery book for the working classes* (Originally published London, 1861, reprinted Whitstable, 1998), pp. 16, 22.
29. BPP 1864 (3416) XXVIII.1, *Sixth report of the medical officer of the Privy Council*, p. 246.
30. Quoted in G. Dunk, *Around St Albans with Geoff Dunk* (St Albans, 1985), p. 47.
31. R. Boyson, *The Ashworth cotton enterprise* (Oxford, 1970), p. 189.
32. Correspondence of the poor law commission with the poor law unions, 1836–47, MH12, 4536 and 4639, the National Archives.
33. Correspondence from Bishop's Stortford and Royston poor law unions to the poor law commissioners, HALS, BG/BIS/1 and BG/ROY/29.
34. Poor law commission report XXIX, 1836, HALS, part 1, p. 144.
35. *Ibid.*
36. K. Griffin, *Transported beyond the seas* (Welwyn Garden City, 1997).
37. *Hertfordshire Mercury*, 'Report on the case of David Warner', 4 September 1875, HALS.
38. Bryant and Baker, *W. Lucas, a Quaker diary*, vol. 1, p. 104.
39. Grey, *Cottage life*, p. 127.
40. J. Lucas, *Phebe's Hitchin book* (Hitchin, 2009), p. 57.
41. Bryant and Baker, *W. Lucas, a Quaker journal*, vol. 1, pp. 138–9.
42. Log book of St Mary's school, Hitchin, HALS, HEd 2/7/15.

Chapter 2

Child labourers in agriculture

Agriculture in Britain

During the Agricultural Revolution, from about 1700 to about 1850, farming generally became more efficient as the use of productive land intensified and the acreage of fallow land was reduced. By 1855 England was regarded as one of the finest agricultural countries and provided employment for many but the agricultural depression of the late 1870s prompted many workers to migrate from the land. By the end of the nineteenth century the use of mechanised machinery such as threshing machines and ploughs had replaced much of the labour-intensive farming that had been practised for centuries.

Agriculture in Hertfordshire

Traditionally, Hertfordshire had always been a farming county. Most of it lies on chalk, overlaid with red clay with flints or boulder clay, with a band of London clay to the south of the county. These geographical variations and the topography of the land have influenced the county's agriculture and the related industries of brewing, malting and straw-plaiting. By 1795 the quantity of corn grown in the centre and north of Hertfordshire had established it as one of the most productive corn-growing counties in the kingdom. Excellent barley, used in the production of malt, was grown in the east of the county and malting was concentrated in the towns of Ware, Stanstead Abbots, Hertford, Sawbridgeworth and Bishop's Stortford. In 1838 twenty of the eighty-two principal maltsters in Hertfordshire worked in Ware. Dark brown malt was used to produce porter, a staple drink of nineteenth-century London.

The close proximity to London and the ever-increasing demands of the capital's markets had influenced Hertfordshire's agriculture from the seventeenth century and shaped the economy of the county. Oats and hay, grown in the centre and south of

Hertfordshire, were vital for London's rapidly growing horse-drawn transport system during the eighteenth and nineteenth centuries. The expanding market garden industry in the Lea Valley supplied fruit and vegetables to local and London markets. In return, Hertfordshire soils were enriched with an almost constant supply of horse manure, soot and the detritus from the tanneries and slaughterhouses of the capital. This was all shipped out from London by barge along the rivers Colne and Lea. Coprolite, a fossil-based fertiliser found near Ashwell, was also used on the land.

Throughout much of the nineteenth century agriculture in Hertfordshire was well-regulated and relatively prosperous. It was flourishing in the middle of the century and was cushioned against the worst effects of the agricultural depression of the late 1870s by its trading links with the capital, although the number of agricultural labourers in Hertfordshire fell from 21,366 in 1861 to 16,877 by 1881 and agricultural workers did face hardship. From the 1860s 73 per cent of the county's farmland was arable and remained so beyond the turn of the century. Farming was organised in different ways across the county, many farmers following four-course (turnips, barley, clover, wheat) or five-course (turnips, barley, clover, clover, wheat) rotations of crops.

'Plenty of work for little money and not much food'

The personal reminiscences of a number of Hertfordshire labourers who worked on the land as children in the 1830s and 1840s were recorded and printed in a 1906 pamphlet published by the Liberal Party to promote free trade and entitled *Steel Dumplings and Barley Spankers.*[1] The memories of these old people set this picture of Hertfordshire agriculture in a human context:

> MR. CARPENTER was a ploughman in those 'Good Old Days' and earned 9s. a week. His wage was for an 8 hours day, but he worked longer, from 4am to 6pm. The principal food of the farm labourers was what they called 'Steel Dumplings' that is flour mixed with water, and boiled. They earned the name of 'Steel Dumplings' because when cooked they were so hard and tough that they could be thrown about without fear of breaking. Another way of eating the dumpling was with vinegar and sugar, when the savoury dish received the name of 'Gooseberry Pudding'. The taste of this was supposed to resemble the gooseberry ... 'Barley Spankers' was another dish. This dish consisted of barley meal mixed with water, fried in fat, when they could get it: otherwise cooked in a frying pan with a little water. Fresh meat they hardly ever saw.

George Brownsell started work at the early age of seven, and earned 3s a week by milking cows and delivering milk in the village. Later on he looked after horses and earned 4s 6d a week. He married when his wages reached the large sum of 9s a week and brought up nine children.

Ralph Miles, of Belsize, Sarratt, is in his eightieth year, and relates how he began work when he was seven years of age. Three years later his wages were advanced from 1s 6d to 2s. and when fifteen earned 4s 6d. He was one of a family of fourteen and when asked how his mother could possibly rear such a family when his father's wages never reached more than 11s a week, he answered 'I really cannot think; it was cruelly hard, we not only had to eat swedes, but we used to cook the rinds of the swedes for food'. Questioned further as to clothing, he said they could rarely afford any, and were dependent on the gifts of those who were better off than themselves. He worked seven days in the week for 1s 6d. 'As for boots' he said, 'my mother used to beg for them, and whatever the sizes were, we had to use them; if too small, our toes had to come outside ... It was often cold, and when the boots were too big it was almost worse; our feet got so sore working in the fields. Of course in those days we did not have boots to fit us like we have today.'

Another Hertfordshire veteran is George Monk, aged seventy-five. 'I went to work when I was but seven. Frightening birds was my job, at 1s 6d a week. Not much money and not a very easy time of it, for I worked seven days a week from 4am to 8pm for some part of the year; 16 hours a day, not ten hours, let alone eight. I was twelve years old before I got 2s a week and I received this for minding cows and selling milk. A few years later I was paid 7s a week 'Not much encouragement to a young man to get married?' I remarked. 'No it wasn't, but I did when I was twenty-four and when I was only getting 10s a week; bread was then 11.5d per loaf.' He further stated that plenty of work for little money and not much food was the condition of the labourer when he was young. When bread was scarce and Monk earned 10s a week, he was often compelled to eat swedes. In talking about the expense of clothing, the genial septuagenarian said, 'I wore a smock frock, inside out all the week and right side up on a Sunday'.

Mr Brownsell was born about 1830, Mr Carpenter in the later 1830s.

Figure 9. Hitchin market in the Bancroft, 1893. A boy stands in front of the shepherd at the sheep pen in the right foreground.

Farmers were usually very influential in their communities, providing employment for skilled workers, labourers and their families. They produced raw materials for individual retailers, millers, corn chandlers and maltsters, and they required the services of skilled craftsmen, blacksmiths, coopers and wheelwrights. It is difficult to estimate how many children the farmers employed throughout the century. In the early years Hertfordshire was certainly an agricultural county where most people lived in rural parishes and worked on the land but by the end of the century 62 per cent of the population lived in the seventeen towns in Hertfordshire with populations of more than 5,000. Even so, and despite the depression that hit agriculture in the second half of the century, there were still many people working on the land in the 1890s including boys aged ten and eleven.

The 1851 census statistics show that about 2,407 children under fifteen were working in some form of agriculture; of these, 174 boys and 7 girls were aged from five to ten. The numbers declined after that; it was estimated that 11 per cent of boys aged from ten to fourteen worked in agriculture in 1861 but less than 4 per cent of that age group were in agriculture in 1891.[2] It is hard to obtain a true picture because so much of the work was part-time or seasonal. Both boys and adults were unemployed for parts of the winter. In 1867 the Employment of Children, Young Persons and Women in Agriculture Commission reported 6 per cent of boys aged from ten to thirteen were unemployed in the winter. In the same report Mrs Fitz-John, wife of a Hertingfordbury agricultural labourer, said that her two boys of ten and twelve years of age looked after

Figure 10. Crabb's farm. It stood in the centre of Hitchin, but was pulled down in the early twentieth century and became the site of the new cattle market. Waitrose supermarket currently occupies the site.

animals in the summer for 2s 6d and 3s a week but would be out of work in the winter, putting a great strain on the family budget.[3]

Most farmers liked to employ mainly boys from a young age, usually seven or eight. The thinking behind this was that starting with simple jobs such as stone-picking, weeding and bird-scaring would quickly accustom them to farm work. They would progress to more demanding jobs such as ploughing and managing horses and carts as their strength increased. This also gave the farmers a ready supply of cheap labour that they were reluctant to forego.

The 1867 commissioners questioned landowners, farmers, vicars and Poor Law officials from parishes mainly in Hatfield, Hertford, Hitchin, Buntingford, St Albans and Ware. Responses were received from the elected Guardians of the Poor who administered the Poor Law Unions. Information about Tewin, Watton, Hertingfordbury, Bengeo and Stapleford came from Guardians in the Hertford Union; about Hitchin and Stevenage from the Hitchin Union; about Ware and Thundridge from the Ware Union; about St Albans and St Stephen's from the St Albans Union; as well as information from the Hatfield and the Buntingford Unions. Mrs Fitz-John was one of the very few people representing labourers or their families whose views reached the commissioners, although most of the other replies from labourers were not printed in the report. One question was whether there should be any restriction on the ages at which children were permitted to work on the land. Three respondents, Mr Abel Smith of Watton, Mr

Sibley an occupier (tenant farmer) of Harpenden and vice-chairman of the St Albans Union Board of Guardians (who also thought that boys between ten and thirteen should attend school and not work on the land in winter) and the Rev. L. Deedes, Rector of Bramfield, believed that no boys should work on the land under ten. This judgement was supported by a formal resolution at a special meeting of the Guardians of the Poor for the Hertford Union, albeit with an escape clause for nine-year-olds that would allow them to work on the land if they had 'a certificate from the manager of the school that they had made sufficient advance in reading and writing to admit of their leaving at that age'. The Rev. Daubeny, rector of Tewin, believed that no boys should go to work before they were eleven or twelve but he was very much in the minority. Mr J.B. Brandram, tenant farmer of Bengeo, said that 'there are certain circumstances connected with growth and education which ought to be taken into consideration with a view to allowing some exceptions' but most respondents believed that it was not desirable to place any restriction on age. Mr Hugh Rayner, tenant farmer of Wallington, asked quite bluntly, 'How is the parent to maintain the children if they remain home till 11 or 12 years of age? They must begin early or they are not fitted for agricultural labourers.' Many of the respondents used the argument that, as they did not themselves employ boys under twelve, there was no need to have a legal restriction at all.

Girls below the age of thirteen or fourteen were rarely employed in Hertfordshire and not at all before the mid-1860s, according to the claims of the Hertfordshire respondents to the 1867 commission. Most respondents considered that one problem was the girls' skirts getting soaked, leading to 'the rheumatics' or other problems, which in turn led to much absenteeism, so it was not thought by farmers to be worth the hassle. Mr Lattimore, a landowner of Wheathampstead, was against the employment of girls or even women because in a wet season they broke down the corn, presumably with their sodden skirts, 'and generally get laid up with colds etc'.[4]

Children under ten usually began by picking up stones. This was done at all times of the year: in winter when the fields were empty of crops and also during ploughing, so that stones did not blunt the plough blades, and in March when the growing corn was beginning to shoot through. Men raked the soil to bring stones to the surface and thus make it easier to pick them up. Two gallon buckets were filled and they became very heavy to lift. The stone-pickers were paid by the load with eighty pails of stones making one load, so that the children had to work long hours to earn much at all. Some children who went to school picked up stones before school and sometimes after school as well. The stones were used to harden the roads and cattle droves. Another job done by children as young as eight was to pull up intractable weeds like charlock and twitch by hand. This often involved children crawling between the growing crops on their hands and knees.

The fully fledged gang system, where a gangmaster controlled a group of workers, children and adults who lived away from home, usually in primitive conditions, and were made to work very long hours for little pay, was prevalent in most East Anglian counties where labour was scattered over large distances. It was little practised in Hertfordshire, a more populated county where labour could easily be recruited locally in times of need. The only involvement of gangs in the county, noted by an inspector in 1867, was that some farmers employed boys under a foreman 'chiefly in pulling charlock or in other light summer work'. Mr Lattimore of Wheathampstead did this, saying that he employed gangs of boys between nine and ten years of age in summer, 'weeding with an overlooker where the land is pestered with charlock and [other] weeds'.[5]

Children of seven or eight worked at bird-scaring or 'keeping crow' as it was sometimes called in the county. It may sound idyllic but it began in February and ended in November. The boys must have been cold and damp, especially in the winter and early spring. They were kept at work all day as Mr Monk testified, even when it got dark, shaking a wooden rattle or a tin containing pebbles or just shouting. Many had inadequate clothing and footwear and often went home cold, weary, hungry, thirsty, often soaking wet and probably looking forward to some company after such a lonely job.

Other employment for young children was to watch the cows, sheep and sometimes pigs. This was quite a popular job as the child could lie down and rest if the animals were grazing contentedly, but sometimes the animals were hard to control, such as pigs scenting acorns and rushing towards the trees. Pigs bent on foraging could be hard, if not impossible, for an eight- or nine-year-old to control.

When boys reached the age of ten or eleven they were generally judged to be capable of becoming ploughboys. Each adult ploughman usually had his ploughboy who first led the horses and later did some ploughing himself. The hours were long, usually from 6am to 6pm with a half hour break at about 10am called 'beaver' and an hour for dinner. The horses would be tired after ploughing about an acre and would be removed from the plough. The men and the boys now had to clean, comb and feed the horses and bed them down for the night. The ploughboy walked many miles up and down the fields. A farmer at Kneesworth, just over the border in Cambridgeshire, told the 1867 commission that a ploughboy of twelve years would 'walk ten miles every day driving the plough in wet, dirty land'.[6]

Boys of ten and eleven were also thought ready to be in charge of horses and often fully laden carts. They were especially in demand at haymaking and harvest time. Boys gathered in the sheaves of corn for the men to set them into stacks ready for carting. During haymaking the carts were piled high as boys led the horses from one haycock to another and then to the place where the haystack was being assembled. Hours were long at harvest time but the reward was more money and beer provided twice a day by the farmer. A boy was usually sent up to the farm to collect the drink and bring it back in a large stone jar.

The evidence for the amounts children were paid is scattered around many sources but what evidence there is for agriculture does not show very high rates and they rose very slowly as the century progressed. However, with the adult wage so low, approximately 9s to 10s at the beginning of the century and maybe 12s to14s by the end, any amount that the children earned might mean the difference between subsisting at home and having to enter the workhouse. This was an ever-present fear in the winter when many men were unemployed for long periods and saw threshing machines taking away their usual employment. Young children at the beginning of the century might receive 8d a day; later they could earn 1s to 1s 6d. Older boys, from ten upwards could earn approximately 2s 6d to 3s 6d a week. Skilled ploughboys might earn 4s or 5s a week by the 1860s. The good times came at harvest when adult labourers were reported to earn 21s a week with beer provided by the farmer; children who stayed working into the evening at harvest had an extra 2d or 3d a day. This extra money was very important to the family economy, providing for expensive items such as boots and tools and payment to a club that might provide some money in hard times or money towards the rent for part of the year.[7]

Accidents involving children

Quite a few accidents, some fatal, were caused by boys being in charge of horses. The roads were comparatively safe for driving carts on but the rutted fields and farm entrances presented great danger, which through inexperience, lack of strength, poor horses or just bad luck caused boys to lose control.

Two newspaper reports of fatal accidents suffered by two eleven-year-old Hertfordshire boys show the dangers of working with horses.

The case of George Fisher, *Hertfordshire Mercury*, 14 September 1867

ROYSTON FATAL ACCIDENT

An inquest was held at the Sun Hotel, Royston, on the 6th instant before T. Sworder Esq., coroner, on the body of George Fisher, a boy 11 years of age. It appeared that the deceased was at work for Mr Vaughn of Royston, carting corn from a field to the farmyard. On the 5th instant he was returning with an empty cart and was riding on the horse's back down a hill. The horse was blind, and for some unknown cause ran up the bank, overturning the cart. The deceased was thrown off and the horse fell upon him, causing instant death. The jury returned a verdict of 'Accidental Death'.

The coroner remarked that an Act had been recently passed for extending the Factory Acts to agriculture and would prevent young persons such as the deceased from being put into positions of danger. The deceased was evidently unable to control the horse and probably endeavouring to stop it, had pulled it onto the bank. He urged upon employers the moral, if not the legal responsibility upon them in seeing that children were not endangering their lives in doing the work allotted to them.

The case of William Phipp, *Hertfordshire Mercury*, 25 July 1868

WATTON SHOCKING AND FATAL ACCIDENT

On Saturday Mr. M.S. Longmore, deputy coroner, held an inquest at the Three Horse Shoes, Datchworth on view of the body of William Phipp, a boy, aged eleven years who was crushed to death by the overturning of a cart he was driving. It appeared from the evidence that the deceased, who was in the service of Mr. Campkin, of Broom Hall Farm, Watton was on the previous day (Friday) employed in carting, being in sole charge of a horse and cart. As he was coming out of the pea field, the horse ran up a bank, and striking against a gatepost, the cart was overturned. The unfortunate boy was thrown down under the shaft and the horse fell upon the shaft so that both the weight of the cart and the horse was upon him. The accident was seen by two labourers at a distance who ran to the spot and found the horse struggling on the top of the poor boy. They raised the horse and the shaft, and on taking up the little fellow, found that he was dead. Mr. Hodges, surgeon, who was sent for, stated that he found the child's chest very much crushed and his right arm broken. He described the turning at the gate, out of which the cart was coming at the time of the accident as dangerous, and said he observed marks where the cart ran up the bank and against the gate post. Mr Campkin said the deceased had been in his service for about eighteen months, and was employed to drive and plough. The horse was quiet and the deceased had orders not to 'run' it; but witness thought that he must have done so to cause the accident. The coroner, in summing up, said it was most improper to place such young boys as the deceased in sole charge of a horse and cart. The jury returned a verdict of 'Accidental death'.

When the Employment of Children, Young Persons and Women in in Agriculture Commission sat again in 1868–69 it sought evidence from the Hertford coroner, Thomas Sworder. He had carried out the inquest on George Fisher and his deputy carried out the inquest on William Phipp. Both boys had died in the farm accidents above. Sworder was not new to child inquests, having conducted one into the case of James Dye, a climbing boy who was suffocated in a flue at Goldings and whose story is told in Chapter 7 (see p. 132). His response to the Assistant Commissioner, George Culley, printed in the final report of the commission, was in note form and included important details not mentioned in the newspaper accounts. The most important was that eleven-year-old boys were too small to reach the halters on the horses' heads; therefore they had no means of stopping the horses. In the case of George Fisher, Sworder noted that the horse was not only blind but also 'an old fly horse', that is one more used previously to pulling a fast light vehicle and therefore 'accustomed to going faster than cart horses usually did'. Fisher had also been at work since 5am and the accident happened at 5pm, when he had been on duty for twelve hours and was 'naturally very tired'. The implication was that he had lost his concentration, quite understandably, through fatigue as the result of working excessively long hours. The farmers escaped guilt because the law, although passed, was not yet in force.[8]

There were cases of non-fatal accidents with horses, including one horrific accident which had a reasonably happy outcome. William Lucas, a Hitchin brewer and Quaker, recorded in his diary in November 1828 that a boy who was ploughing was thrown down by the horses and, presumably, kicked and trampled on so badly that his intestines hung out of the gash in his side. The surgeon Frederick Hawkins was called, replaced the boy's intestines, and sewed up the boy's side without anaesthetic. Lucas reported that 'he is now in a fair way to recovery'. The boy must have been tough, brave and lucky to have survived such an experience. Non-fatal accidents with horses were quite common; for example, Potten End School log book recorded that Stephen Day was absent, 'having been kicked on the arm by a horse'.

Working with horses and other animals was not the only danger for boys working on farms. Working with farm implements and machinery could also be hazardous. Charles Titmuss was away from Pirton School because he lost the thumb of his right hand, cut off by a chaff cutter, and a boy called Gibbon was absent from St Mary's School, Ware in 1868, having received a severe thrust in his arm from a pitchfork.[9]

Children did many other jobs, depending on the area in which they lived; sometimes they helped adults like the shepherd or went pea- and potato-picking, gathered acorns and ferns for the pigs, cared for the turkeys, drilled turnips and peeled osiers. The old system of engaging agricultural workers for the year at farms had virtually died out by the 1860s and most adults and children who worked on the land were hired and paid by the week or for piece work. A few boys were taken on as 'backhouse boys' to live in the farmhouses and do many chores in the house, such as cleaning knives, or in the farmyard. For this they would receive their keep and maybe 20s a quarter.

Schooling

School log books like that of St Mary's, Hitchin, show how disruptive agricultural work of all kinds could be to schooling. The long holiday in the summer was called the Harvest Vacation and started with little formal notice; when attendance dropped to a certain level the time for the holiday chose itself. It was more a capitulation than an announcement – an acceptance of the inevitable. The start date varied from place to place and from school to school, according to the readiness of the crop for harvesting. At such times children who had had regular attendance could be absent when the opportunity arose to earn money for pea- or potato-picking. The farmers' demand for acorns at 1s a bushel meant a further opportunity to earn a small sum. Haymaking led to more absence. Sometimes the local gentry employed young lads as 'beaters' or 'bashers' at their shoots. This practice continued into the 1890s and in that decade some of the gentry were gently reprimanded by the school attendance committees for employing ten-year-olds who should have been at school.

The following extracts from the two pages that survive from an excuse book of Chorleywood School, the log book of Flaunden School and the Ware Board of Guardians' school attendance committee show excuses for non-attendance and illustrate the illegal employment of school children.

Extracts from the excuse book of Chorleywood School, June 1866

George Wallington	Went wooding
Emily Robinson	Mind the baby
M. Wallington	Went wooding
Sophie Wallington	Went wooding
J. Basting and Jos	Work
W.H. and M.Weedon	Work
J. Roberts	Chaff Cutting

In addition to these entries for Chorleywood School, the names of five other children were entered with the single word 'permission' against their names, from which it can be inferred that the parents sought permission for absence and that it was granted. This suggests that it was more about relations between the parents and the school than about enforcing attendance. It may be further inferred that most of the 'permissions', sought and granted, were for similar reasons to those recorded against the names of the 'miscreants'.

Extracts from the log book of Flaunden School, 1868–9

April 1868	The attendance had not been so good during this [week]. Many of the children have been gathering dandelions [used for preparing medicines] this week.
September 1868	The attendance this week has been very low indeed owing to many of the children gleaning.
October 1868	Attendance better, still some away for acorn gathering.
October 1868	Several elder ones away to gather acorns.
August 1873	Albert and William Gutteridge away for work.
August 1873	Joseph Goodman away for work.
September 1879	Attendance rather low through the week, several children being away for gleaning.

Extract from the Ware Board of Guardians school attendance minute book for 23 April 1878

Mr Blackaby presented a list of children not attending school and directions were given that the parents be warned. Mr Blackaby also stated that the under-mentioned children were employed contrary to the Act:

W. Blendall	9 years, employed by Capt. Trower
John Ward	11 years, employed by Mr Woodhouse
R. Woodhouse	10 years, employed by Mr Woodhouse
L Warner	11 years, employed by Mr Bugg
S.W Warner	9 years, employed by Mr Teal
Albert Pedder	10 years, employed by Mr Ashford

The following extract shows that even as late as 1891 Ware Board was still having to pursue people who employed young boys to beat for game and it seems that Captain Trower had not been dissuaded from this practice.

Extract from the Ware Board of Guardians committee book for 15

December 1891

The school attendance officer reported that Capt. Trower had employed Thomas Gollop aged 10 and Charles Turner aged 10 on the [date not given]inst at Stanstead and Mr Smith Bosanquet had employed William Bell aged nine and [first name not shown] Woods aged 11 on the [date not given]inst looking for game.

The clerk was instructed to write to Capt. Trower and Mr Smith Bosanquet and call their attention to sections 5 and 6 of the 1870 Education Act which enacted that anyone employing a child in contravention of the Act is liable to a penalty.[10]

Children were kept off school to carry food to their parents in the fields or mind the younger children if their mothers were working on the land. In one case at Potten End in 1866 a boy was kept at home every morning to fetch milk for the family.[11] When there had been a bad storm or high winds overnight, children were kept off school to go wooding, that is to pick up wood that had been blown down and could be added to the family's wood stack to eke out the fuel supplies in readiness for winter fires.

An activity that had a big impact on the families' food supplies and on school attendance was gleaning. It was very important, as the flour that was produced from the gleaned wheat could be made to last through the autumn and into the winter. The villagers were allowed to go into the fields after the harvest was gathered in to pick up the ears of wheat that had been left on the ground. Usually all the children except the smallest were pressed into service. Each group had its part of the field and a bell was rung to signal that gleaning could begin. Sometimes disputes broke out as this piece of doggerel from Welwyn shows:

Here gleaners fight
With stones and scratches to maintain their right.[12]

Schools appreciated how important gleaning, which went on for two or three weeks, was to the family economy and sometimes extended the holiday to accommodate the gleaners. Norton School opened again in September 1894 after seven weeks, not the usual five or six, because gleaning had not finished within the five weeks allowed for the harvest holiday. It was of little use to try to get the children back into school while the families were still in the fields. The Wareside school log book of 1881 shows that when the school re-opened after the Harvest Vacation, 'very few children were present all the week in consequence of the gleaning not being over'.[13] There can be little doubt that, like absence for straw-plaiting, the pattern of rural employment had an adverse effect on the children's education. It is difficult to regard the actions of the parents, concerned to keep their families alive and out of the workhouse, as anything but highly practical with a strong sense of priorities even if it did leave their children largely uneducated. Teachers complained that the children soon forgot what they had learnt. This was especially true of those children who went to work in the fields for three to six months and then came back to school in times of unemployment.

Many farmers saw little merit in their ploughboys and cart drivers having more than a very basic education and pointed to night schools and Sunday schools, which did not interfere with work, as ways of making up any deficiency. The 1870 Education Act made the National schools in the villages look at their practices as they had to improve before they received the government grant, still based on attendance and test results. In 1871 the vicar of North Mymms considered how to improve the attendance at the Boys' School at Welham Green. He summed up the problem: 'On the one hand the farmer must not have the supply of his labour market lessened and on the other the poor man [a farm labouring father] cannot afford to lose the little help that his boys of ten or eleven ... are ... able to give him.' The vicar agreed a plan with the farmers. What the schoolmaster thought of it is not recorded.

The plan was that, firstly, apart from haymaking and harvest, boys from six to twelve could go to work in the fields only if the schoolmaster sent them; secondly, the schoolmaster had to keep a list of children whose parents wished them to go bird-scaring and the like. They would be allowed out of school no more than two days in any week, the farmers notifying the schoolmaster when they needed help. This arrangement lasted for two years and then the vicar had to adopt the official regulations that no child under ten was to be employed by the farmers and children from ten to twelve had to be in school for at least seventy-five days a year. These children were known as half-timers. After 1880 children who had passed the test for standard four could leave school to go to work full-time.[14] The National Agricultural Union argued that abundant and cheap child labour enabled farmers to keep adult wages low. Certainly the nearer to London the agricultural labourers were, the higher their wages, and probably those of the children too, as there was more competition from employers in other industries for their services.

Even in 1890, ten years after legislation had made school compulsory, the Tewin School log book recorded the cry of many parents, 'The child can earn a little money. We are very poor and sadly need it, and so I must have a boy kept away in the hay field for a week or two.'[15]

Housing

The housing of agricultural workers was, with a few exceptions, as inadequate as most other accommodation for the labouring poor. What today are very desirable cottages in Hertfordshire villages were throughout the nineteenth century usually damp, dilapidated and overcrowded. Some landlords in what were known as closed parishes, where one landlord owned most of the housing stock, did provide good housing for their workers and tried to make sure that families that might be a burden to the parish were excluded from the village. One employer who provided cottages that were described by the rector of Stapleford in 1867 as first rate was Mr Abel Smith of Woodhall Park. He tried to make sure that cottages were not overcrowded by placing restrictions on the number of people living in them, discouraging the taking in of lodgers. Good water and gardens for growing vegetables were provided and the cottages were well-ventilated.[16] In contrast, a report on cottages in Walkern by Dr Ogle, Medical Officer of Health for the Hertford Union, stated that they were filthy, ill-ventilated and that typhoid raged in the village. He wryly noted that his predecessor had died from the disease. He also found that in one cottage in which a family called Carter lived seven people had to sleep in one bedroom, although by the time he got there one had died of typhoid. In another cottage a woman, her three sons aged eighteen, fourteen and ten, as well as two daughters aged twelve and ten, all slept in one room. Ogle estimated that in twelve cottages there were fifteen bedrooms in which eighty-four people slept. It is not surprising that the small windows were rarely opened as there were usually beds close up to them and people had a horror of draughts. Some windows were jammed shut and could not be opened. The water supply from some of the Walkern wells was disgusting, some of it quite yellow. The overcrowding was just as bad in downstairs rooms. In the living room of one Pirton cottage where a family of thirteen lived only the girls were able to sit down; the boys stood against the wall. It is no wonder that the father sometimes took refuge in the local tavern where he could sit down in some comfort.[17]

These were the conditions in which many children had to live. It is no wonder that in Walkern, a village of about 800 people, 50 deaths were reported in 36 months from 1873

Figure 11. Agricultural labourers, as well as sweeps and straw-plaiters, lived in Hollow Lane, Hitchin. Open country is visible at the top of the picture.

to 1875. This overcrowded, insanitary sort of accommodation was to be found in many other villages. Rural Sanitary Committee minutes described bad conditions, such as the open ditch running down the main street of Hertingfordbury, which contained both rain water and sewage.[18] In 1867 Mr Peck, the relieving officer of the Hertford Union, said that the worst cottages in his district were in Aston, Datchworth and Bennington and the best belonged to Abel Smith. At Wheathampstead Mr Lattimore said that 'modern cottages run up by builders on speculation are very small and crowded'. At Shephall there were six cottages with one bedroom each and for water most villagers had to go to the parsonage pump. The rents were from 1s 6d to 1s 8d a week. Mr Strickland, the relieving officer of the Hitchin Union, wrote in 1867 that in his area the labourers' cottages were generally in open villages where there was usually no principal landowner and many of them were in a very bad state. The worst were in the back lanes of Baldock and Hitchin where the agricultural labourers and their families lived, and at Stevenage, Weston and Clothall. He ended on a more favourable note, saying that the cottages in Codicote were very good and that Mr Hancock was building very good ones at Willian.[19]

Children lived in insanitary conditions at home, often suffering from chilblains and rheumatics, and with inadequate clothing and footwear to withstand the worst of the weather. Often the only protection they had from the rain was an old sack thrown over their shoulders. There was always the threat of an outbreak of fever if they lived in one of the villages with the worst housing and periods of malnutrition if their fathers were out of work in the winter and the children could not find employment either. There were, however, a few advantages for these child workers in agriculture, compared to their counterparts in other work. In the spring, after the last of the frosts, and in the summer it was a fairly healthy life in the open air and they had more freedom than, for example, chimney-climbing boys or the children in the silk and paper mills.

Endnotes

1. R.J. Childs, *Testimony and portraits of men and women living in Hertfordshire, who suffered by protection in the good old days* (Watford, 1906), HALS photocopy in pamphlet file 1 on agriculture.
2. BBP, statistical tables issued after each census, 1841–91, which include breakdown of occupations by age, HALS.
3. BPP 1867–8 (4068) XVII.1 and 1868–9 (4202) XIII.1, *Commission on the employment of children, young persons and women in agriculture* (1867).
4. *Ibid.*
5. *Ibid.*
6. *Ibid.*
7. Young, *Agriculture of Hertfordshire*; BPP 1861 (2895) LXII.397, *Miscellaneous statistics of the United Kingdom, part III, pp. 271–3.*
8. BPP 1868–9 (4202) XIII.1.
9. Pirton school log book, HALS, HEd/1/83/2; St Mary's, Ware school log book, D/P 116.
10. Chorleywood school excuse book, HALS, HEd/1/193; Flaunden school log book, HALS, HEd/1/111/1; Ware board of guardians school attendance committee minute books for 1878 and 1891, HALS, BG/WAR/102.
11. Potten End school log book.
12. S. Allen (ed.), *W. Branch Johnson's articles on Hertfordshire history* (Codicote, undated), p. 8.
13. Norton school log book, 1894, HALS, HEd /44/2; Wareside school log book, 1881, HALS, HEd/113/4.
14. P. Kingsford, *North Mymms schools and their children, 1700–1964* (originally published Hatfield, 1987, reprinted 1999), p. 19.
15. Quoted in S. James (ed.), *Tewin school*, p. 19.
16. BPP 1867–8 (4068) XVII.1, evidence on Watton.
17. Quoted in J. Wayne (ed.), *A foot on three daisies* (Pirton, 1987), p. 100.
18. J. Cussans, *History of Hertfordshire*, three volumes, grangerised edn (Hertford, 1880), vol. 3, p. 133, HALS, D/ECU/3; Hertfordshire Mercury, December 1875.
19. BPP 1867–8 (4068) XVII.1.

Chapter 3

The straw plait trade

Origins

The process of plaiting straw into strips to be sewn into hats developed in Tuscany from the fourteenth century. By the seventeenth century the straw plait trade had spread to Switzerland, Austria, Germany and England. The expansion of the trade in this country was probably influenced by refugee Flemish workers settling in Hertfordshire and Bedfordshire, where soil and climatic conditions for growing wheat with a tall straight stem suitable for plaiting were favourable. By the middle of the nineteenth century it had become a lucrative seasonal trade, meeting the demand for hats, baskets and footwear.

The British straw-plaiting trade

By 1719 the straw-plaiting trade of the south Midlands, including Hertfordshire and Bedfordshire, was well established. In 1732 straw-plaiting was regarded as an almost entirely female occupation, requiring little strength but much dexterity, and an eminently 'useful employment for the poor in workhouses'.[1] Throughout the eighteenth century the trade gradually expanded to rival the other domestic industries of wool-spinning and lace-making but those who could afford it preferred the straw hats fashioned from the delicate plaits produced in Leghorn and other parts of Italy. The English straw plait, known as wholestraw, was thicker and produced a cruder product. The trade began to flourish in Britain at the turn of the nineteenth century, partly because of restricted imports during the Napoleonic Wars (1800–15) and because of the introduction of new plaiting techniques. The invention of a 'chine' or 'cheen', a small hand-held straw splitter, enabled British straw-plaiters to split lengths of straw into different thicknesses. Various people claimed to have invented the tool but it was in widespread use by 1803.[2] The use of finer straws or 'splints'

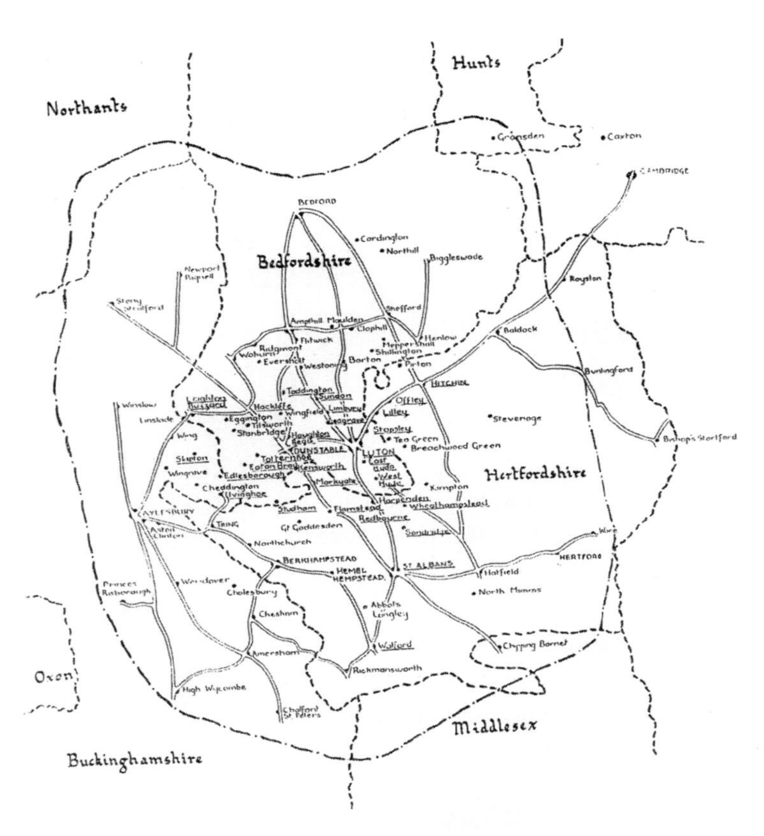

Figure 12. The plait-making areas in and around Hertfordshire.

enabled plaiters to produce a better quality plait with more intricate designs. This happened at a time when supplies of Italian plait were cut off by the English blockade of foreign ports so the trade in this country increased dramatically. Changes in fashion and the size of hats affected the trade throughout the century, as an increase of just five centimetres to a hat brim required twice as much straw to be plaited. In 1820 the number of straw hats made for the British market was 71,629, rising to 274,906 in 1828 and falling to 4,995 in 1842.

Traditionally the prosperity of the straw plait trade fluctuated, influenced by the quantity and quality of home-produced and imported plait as well as fashion. The profitable trade of the mid-1860s, when over 100,000 kg of straw was used for the home market, started to decline from 1869 when Chinese plait was imported, to be followed by considerable quantities of Japanese plait from 1891. From the mid-1870s legislation governing children's employment and schooling also started to affect the

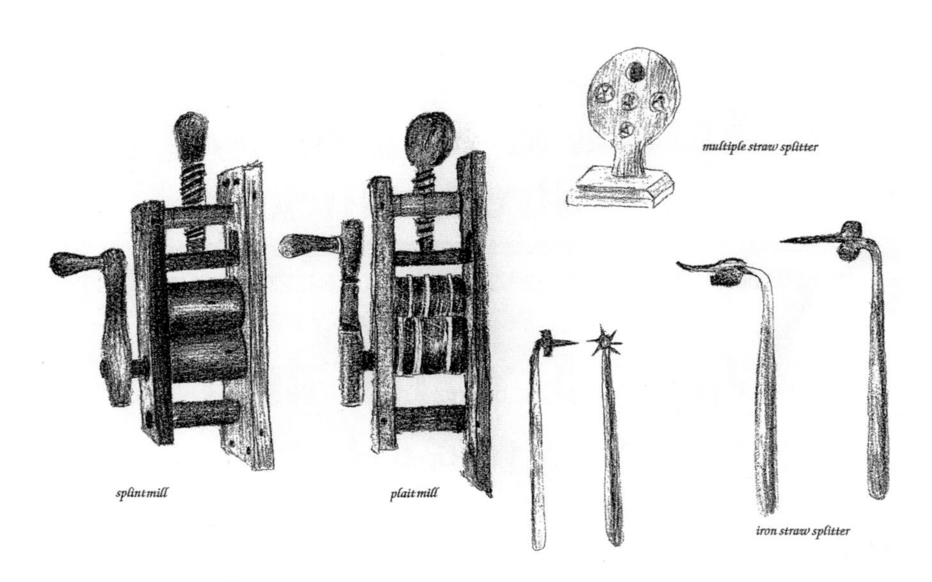

Figure 13. The simple tools used for straw-plaiting.

trade. The Workshops Regulations Act of 1867 banned children under the age of eight from working in handcrafts, including straw-plaiting, and required children between the ages of eight and thirteen to attend elementary school for at least ten hours a week, as 'part-timers'. At first the law was routinely avoided, as the younger children in plaiting schools slipped out of the back door when factory inspectors called. By 1875 children were more likely to attend elementary school, partly because cases of non-attendance were successfully challenged and partly because the straw plait trade had declined to such an extent that child labour was no longer profitable. The introduction of sewing machines into the straw hat trade from 1877 changed the nature of demand for straw plait. Chinese plait was cheap and there was a rising demand for cheap straw hats produced by machine. English straw-plaiters, like those in Italy, found prices for their finished product fell markedly and it was not worthwhile to produce plait. The English plaiters did not riot as their Italian counterparts did but tried to find other means of making money.

The straw plait trade in Hertfordshire

The trade of straw-plaiting is known to have existed in Hertfordshire from the seventeenth century. This was partly due to the fact that the best wheat for straw-plaiting grew on the chalky, dry soils of the Chilterns, to the north and west around Hertfordshire. Several varieties of wheat were grown, Dugdale, Golden Drop, Chittam

PLAIT MART,
Back Street, Hitchin.

PLAIT BOUGHT DAILY at MARKET PRICE,
and Money Paid ON DELIVERY.

HOURS & DAYS FOR BUYING:

MONDAY, 3 to 6 o'clock.
TUESDAY, 9 to 1 o'clock.
WEDNESDAY, 3 to 5 o'clock.
THURSDAY & FRIDAY, 2 to 6.
SATURDAY, 9 to 1 o'clock.

PLAIT to be DOUBLED in HALF-YARDS, & delivered
in not less than TEN YARDS.

NO PLAIT RECEIVED FROM CHILDREN.

JOHN J. WORKER, MANAGER.

AUGUST, 1874.

CHARLES HOLMES, "JOURNAL" OFFICE, BRAND STREET, HITCHIN.

Figure 14. A notice of 1874 about Hitchin plait market, one of the largest in Hertfordshire.

or Chiddam White and Red Lammas and these provided a ready supply for straw-plaiters. Markets for the sale of plait became established along the main roads from London, at St Albans on Watling Street, at Hemel Hempstead and Tring. Straw-plaiting was known as a trade in Harpenden, Watford and Rickmansworth. By 1804 the straw plait trade was also established in the Hertfordshire towns of Hitchin, Stevenage, Hatfield, Redbourn and Berkhamsted. As the century progressed the trade expanded rapidly into a lucrative cottage industry throughout many of the villages in the north and west of the county, such as Pirton, the Wymondleys and St Ippolyts, and some to the west and south such as Potten End, Wheathampstead and North Mymms.

It was a seasonal trade, which could be lucrative while it lasted during the peak months of December to May, but earnings depended on the quality of the finished plait and the availability of flourishing markets. The largest market was at Hitchin (Tuesday), but others were at Hemel Hempstead (Thursday), Tring (Friday) and St Albans (Saturday). Many plaiters walked considerable distances to the markets where the prices for finished work were usually higher than those offered by the plait dealers who travelled throughout the county. The trade was dependent on the straw hat trade, which was also seasonal. Factories for making up the plait into hats were set up in Hertford and St Albans in the 1830s. In the 1840s there were also smaller outlets in Redbourn and Harpenden. In 1834 Brazilian hats made of palm leaves were produced at St Albans and at Redbourn where the census returns of 1851 show children and young people from the age of five working in the trade. The Brazilian hat trade failed in about 1870 but hat factories in St Albans turned to making 'boater hats' for men until the turn of the century.

The availability of child labour to fulfil the demands of the market became important as the trade expanded and the earnings of accomplished child straw-plaiters were of considerable benefit to their families. In 1804 it was claimed that children in Redbourn earned 8s weekly after only six weeks of tuition but this figure may be exaggerated.[3] Evidence from Parliamentary papers in 1818 stated that in straw-plaiting families the 'wife and children can often earn more than the husband'. Most of the husbands were labourers whose wages throughout the nineteenth century never rose above about 13s a week. In 1837 a child plaiting for eight or nine hours daily generally earned 8d a week when aged eight, increasing to 1s aged nine, 1s 6d aged ten, 1s 9d aged eleven and to 2s by the age of twelve. From the age of sixteen they could expect to earn 3s 6d a week. In 1843 boys and girls aged from eight to thirteen earned about 18d a week after paying for their schooling at the plait school although younger children hardly earned enough to pay for their schooling and straw. In 1864 they might earn 7d for a score of plait, but this excluded the cost of the straw they had purchased.

While it lasted the straw plait trade was the most significant cottage industry in Hertfordshire, playing a very important part in village life. At the height of the trade hundreds, if not thousands, of young children in Hertfordshire were plaiting. The 1851 census shows that 25 per cent of all plaiters were under the age of fifteen, 708 aged between five and ten, and 1,489 aged between ten and fourteen. There were also 337 hat-makers, all female, of whom 49 were under ten. By 1861 64 per cent (387) of all male plaiters in Hertfordshire were boys aged from five to ten and 20 per cent (1,705) were girls aged between five and fourteen, including 480 aged from five to ten. In 1871 some 303 boys and 1,939 girls aged from five to fourteen were plaiting. The trade then declined so rapidly that by 1881 the census returns show no children in Hertfordshire under ten as plaiters, but older children were still working long hours in the straw hat trade.[4]

Children working as straw-plaiters and plait schools

Straw-plaiting differed from other forms of child labour in the county. No large machinery was used, only a hand-held straw splitter, and small splint and plait mills (small machines to flatten the straw). It could be done at home, at school, or while talking to friends and neighbours by children from the age of two upwards. It was not factory owners who compelled children to start plaiting at such an early age. It was their parents who, influenced by economic necessity or sometimes greed, believed that when they were old enough to 'sit still and be kept quiet', children should be 'set to the plait' at a plaiting school. The plaiting school system was a form of caretaking of young children while their parents worked, with the bonus that the children's earnings were a welcome addition to the weekly wages of their family. Child straw-plaiters used no mechanised tools, but in the workshops known as 'plaiting schools' they too were watched as closely as the children in the silk and paper mills who worked to the constant rhythm and clatter of machinery.

The plaiting schools were different from the 'reading' or 'day' schools found in many Hertfordshire towns and villages. Parents paid on average 2d a week for each child to attend and they generally supplied the straw for plaiting that their children used in the school. Children from the ages of two to fourteen usually attended, but in 1864 a report to Parliament stated that children as young as one attended plaiting schools and that a two year old was actually plaiting. Boys tended to leave earlier than girls; boys left if farm work was available locally, while in the St Albans area girls might leave to work in the straw hat factories from the age of ten or twelve.

The plaiting schools were usually run by a local woman, the plaiting mistress, in her own home. Little attempt was made to teach the children anything except plaiting although there might be some attempt to teach reading by repeating a few verses from the Bible or from a hymn. Many parents chose plaiting schools where the mistress was strict with the children, keeping them working until they had finished the amount that the parents had set them to do, and using a cane if the children faltered or lost interest in their work.

The schools generally were not pleasant places. Tightly packed into confined spaces, children sat on little benches or stools, or anywhere they could squeeze in. Sometimes there were as many as eighteen children in a room seven feet square. With restricted ventilation the rooms became stuffy and offensive, and children were often pale and wan from being cooped up in such enclosed places. They suffered from bronchial ailments, coughs and colds, sores at the corners of their mouths and stomach problems, possibly caused by hunger and by constantly putting bleached or dyed straw between their lips. The rooms were often too congested to allow fires to be lit, but as the children could not plait if they were cold, they sometimes had a 'dicky pot' to keep their feet warm. Mrs Gregory of Bovingdon wrote about the girls arranging their petticoats around the stools on which they sat, so that no smoke could harm the plait. The 'dicky pots' were made of earthenware filled with hot embers of wood or coal and were tucked underneath the girls' long skirts. Inspectors claimed that the smoke from the 'dicky pots' added to the already foul atmosphere of the schools. The use of these devices was inherently dangerous and there were stories of children being burned to death, but surprisingly no such accidents seem to have been recorded in Hertfordshire, although a girl's death in Potten End may have been caused by this practice. Certainly there was a fatal accident of this kind at Chesham just over the border in Buckinghamshire.[5]

These extracts from the Second Report of the Children's Employment Commission in 1864 reveal much about Hertfordshire plait schools.[6]

Berkhamsted

Mrs Norris's Straw Plait School

The room is irregular shape but equal as possible to 12 feet square, and only 6ft 3 in high. With the average number of children the allowance is only 43 cubic feet for each person. It has been as low as 29.

Mrs Norris [said] 'My average number of children is 20 but I have had 30. Most of them plait but the youngest do nothing and are only sent to be kept quiet. They begin to plait here about 5 years old. School is from 8.45am till 12 and 1 till 4. Four are waiting behind now (to finish their work). The little one there, 5 years old, is standing to work because he is tired of sitting down and will soon be going at 4.30pm. It is quite the outside that I reckon to keep any. The fever took off a good many here a few months ago'.

Mrs Hancock's Straw Plait School

Mrs Hancock [said] 'I keep only a night plait school, viz. from 5pm till 8 and have usually about 10 children all from 5 to 10 years old. Some of them go to other plait schools or reading schools in the day time before they come to me. If they have not done their work I have to keep them perhaps a quarter of an hour over their time. I have the big stick to frighten them, but I do not like to use it. One boy, 10 years, does eight yards each evening here, but he is very quick. My girl, who is eleven, cannot do five yards of the same plait. It is worth about 7d a score. Sometimes half the money goes for [buying] the straw and I should think that with children's work that is about the average'. The inspector wrote 'there are a number of straw plait schools in the town; I should think almost a dozen. The day school hours are from 9am till 12 and from 1 till 4. At these the children have to read either once or twice a day for a few minutes. About 5 is the general age to begin plait here, not much younger, although one or two at 4. At about 14 or fifteen they leave school and work at home'.

The views of a child from a different school, Sarah Ann Meagher, aged 7 years

She said, 'I go to Scott's plait school three times a day, viz from 8.30 till 12 and from 1 till 4 and from 5 till 8pm. Mother sets me five yards to do in each school, one yard at dinner and one yard at tea time. Sometimes I have to get up at 7 or 6.30 and begin work, but I never did any after coming from school at night. If I do "five" mother says I'm a good girl; she doesn't hit me, the mistress does sometimes.'

The inspector added a note, 'I saw this girl along the street with another plaiting on their way from school at tea time'.

Mrs Gates's Straw Plait School

[The inspector wrote] 'At this school only a few were present, but only two answered to the question of having been to a reading school for a year, one for two.'

Martha Gates [said] 'I keep a plait school for my mother, and usually have about 14 children here. I teach them reading and hymns. The youngest Harriet Gates, now 4 years and 5 months old, comes to both school times, viz. 9 till 12 and 1 till 5; I have no school in the evening. Only two or three of them, I think, have been to the reading school, and those but for a short time. Besides the two that have said that they went, one may have been for two or three weeks perhaps.'

[The inspector interpolates] 'A girl at another place afterwards told me of having been at school with a child of only two years plaited in the last winter twelvemonth. On asking her name I found it to be the child Harriet Gates.'

Mrs Watts. Examined 6 May

Mr Watts [said] 'Not a plaiter myself; keep a small school; had three children of my own and four scholars; come at six and leave at four; and an hour allowed for dinner. In my judgement I think the mothers task the children too much; the mistress is obliged to make them perform it; otherwise they would put them to other schools. I think the children are put too early to work, it stops their growth. I teach my own children sewing and reading as well as plaiting and have offered to teach the scholars who come to my school, but the parents care nothing for it and plaiting alone is everything with them; grown up girls have no more idea of sewing, or making a shift for themselves, than a baby. In Hempstead it is too much the case that married men, knowing their wives and families earn enough to support themselves by plaiting, take no care of them and spend all their earnings at the beer-houses.'

The plait schools were open for long hours, from 8am to 5pm with an hour for lunch and, for children over six years old, an evening class from 6pm to 8 or 9pm. In some villages, for example Bourne End, there was also a Saturday plaiting school. If their parents could afford to pay the fees, children attended the plait schools whenever they had straw to plait. During the hours of winter darkness the schools were lit by a single tallow candle or a rush light placed on a stand in the centre of the room. Children also plaited at home by candlelight, sometimes beyond 11pm or midnight, especially if there was work to be completed for market day. Edwin Grey of Harpenden, writing about the 1860s, says that when the children became adept at their work they could tell by feel when to put in a new piece of straw without having to look and could plait as well by firelight as in broad daylight.[7]

Generally, by the age of four, if not earlier, children were thought to have acquired the basic skills, and be able to plait their 'ten' (ten yards) a day. By the age of six this might increase to fifteen yards and to seventeen yards a day by the age of seven. Children had to plait almost constantly from the time they got up to the time they went to bed to achieve this amount. Children aged nine or ten might plait for between twelve and fourteen hours a day.

The process of straw-plaiting and the involvement of children

The ideal wheat for straw-plaiting was a valuable crop, carefully chosen by farmers and straw dealers. It had to be tall, straight, and free from disease or blemish. When ripe it was usually cut by hand by a skilled itinerant worker or a local thatcher before being bound into sheaves. Local families, such as the Flittons of Flamstead mentioned by Edwin Grey, specialised in the delicate work of cutting the wheat for straw-plaiting so that it was not bruised.[8]

Once the wheat chosen for straw-plaiting had been harvested the longest straws were chosen from the sheaf and the head of corn cut off. Any leaves or knots were then stripped away, leaving clean straws that were cut into lengths of nine inches. These lengths were graded by the thickness of the straw stem, using a series of circular metal sieves mounted in a wooden frame, before being tied into small bundles, prepared and sold to plaiters. Before being plaited, the straws were prepared by being bleached for several hours in wash tubs or boxes containing a quantity of charcoal sprinkled with brimstone or sulphur to preserve the straw and produce a whiter plait. Straw was also coloured with vegetable and wood dyes. Occasionally this was done by the plaiters themselves but the process was usually done by the dealers and sold in bundles ready to plait. From 1857 the limited range of colours was considerably extended as aniline dyes, made from indigo distilled with caustic soda, were introduced. Once bleached or dyed, the straws were split vertically into between three and nine splints, using a small hand-held straw splitter. Finally, the splints were flattened in a splint mill to make them more flexible before plaiting.

Starting to plait was difficult, as was the 'setting in' of new splints to continue the pattern. It required nimble, dextrous fingers. Children used their thumbs and second fingers to hold the plait and their forefingers to turn the splints. There were numerous plait patterns to learn. Children started with the simplest plait, 'Dunstable Twist', a flat pigtail design made with whole straws, before attempting more intricate patterns. Each village or town might specialise in several designs such as: medium twist (Hitchin); fine split Devon and moss edge (Chesham); china pearl and Coburg rock (Berkhamsted); pearl, bird's eye and whipcord (Harpenden). To help themselves remember the pattern sequences of different designs, and to relieve the dreary monotony, the children chanted rhymes as they worked:

> Under one and over two
> Put it tight and that will do.
> Or
> Criss-cross patch and then a twirl
> Twist it back for an English Pearl.

As the work progressed they looped it over their left arm, leaving the sharp ends of the splints sticking out from the pattern. Clipping these ends off required a delicate touch if

Figure 15. Examples of straw plait. From the top, Dunstable improved, English wholestraw, English rustic, diamond and wave. The last three examples are of Italian-made plait.

the straw was to be sold later. Children from about three years old laboriously practised on unsellable plait work, 'widdle-waddle', clipping as many as ten yards in a day before attempting plait intended for sale. When the required length of patterned plait was completed, it was pressed through a wooden plait mill, similar to a splint mill, except with grooved rollers so that the edge of the finished pattern was not flattened. Finished plait was measured in yards and sold in scores (twenty yards) or fractions of scores.

Not all straw-plaiting was done in plait schools. Much was done in the open air and in good weather plaiters walked along or stood and gossiped at doorways. Some plaiters worked in their own homes and many were accused of being slovenly housekeepers because they did not spend all day on household tasks. It was, however, in their interests to keep the house as clean as possible, so that the plait was not spoilt and the best prices would be obtained. The trimming of the plait meant that pieces of straw would be strewn over the floor and could be swept up at the end of day to be used as bedding for animals. Many women and children got up early to do essential housework and to leave the rest of the day for plaiting. It was said that:

> Straw plaiters are up in the morning betimes
> Get the odd jobs done before the sun shines.

Some middle-class commentators, especially clergymen, stressed that straw-plaiting could lead to immorality, especially as boys and girls walked through the countryside together plaiting unsupervised and girls earned money for themselves and were therefore less under the control of their parents. The figures on illegitimate births do not bear out this contention in most areas, with the illegitimacy rates for straw-plaiters usually no higher than those of the population as a whole. It was probably more a case of a vivid imagination and righteous indignation on the part of the commentators than reality. The thought of losing control over the young girls who could earn enough to spend a little on themselves was one which the clergy, especially, found hard to countenance. The log book of Potten End School gives numerous examples of girls staying at home to plait to earn extra money for new Easter bonnets or summer clothes.[9]

In 1843 a factory inspector visited plaiting schools at a time when the trade was depressed and reported on three counties together, as conditions were so similar in all three; as well as Hertfordshire, his reports covered the adjacent counties of Buckinghamshire and Bedfordshire. They were made public in the Second Report of the Employment of Children Commission.

The inspector reported:[10]

> The elder girls and boys above ten years are set tasks of about ten hours; the tasks of the younger vary from five to eight hours: when they first begin they only work a short time at once; the tasks are generally, or at least can be, done by six pm; but in cases of idleness and their set task not being done they are detained till it be finished.
>
> This plaiting is a complete bar to anything like education, for as soon as children can use their fingers they are put to it. At Chesham repeated attempts have been vainly made to establish schools; parents will not send their children to a place where in lieu of gaining anything they are obliged to pay something.

> Young persons of both sexes are engaged in it; and as in summer they take their work into fields and congregate much together, the usual consequence of such intercourse ensues, and chastity is at a sad discount, while prostitution is at a high premium. This was the opinion of every one I conversed with on the subject. The Rev. Mr Payne, of Chesham, in answer to educational queries, says, 'I have already intimated, and I do it with regret, that the religious and moral condition of some of the youths in this town is painfully distressing; fornication is lamentably frequent'.
>
> Though, in this respect, their moral condition is very low indeed as members of the community they are a very orderly and well-behaved class.
>
> It is stated by medical witnesses that the children are put to this work from three years old and upwards; that they are engaged in it from the time they rise till they go to bed; and that, from the crowded state of the rooms, the want of exercise and the long abstinence from food, they become sickly and more than commonly subject to stomach and catarrhal diseases.
>
> The silk manufacturers in Herts and Bucks, who are under the Act [specifying that no child under eight be employed] complain much of their trade being injured by the early age at which plaiters commence work. By the time they are old enough to be employed in these works they can earn as much or more than they [the silk mill owners] at first can afford to pay; and such is the preference for the straw plait, as being less restrained, that they continue in it even on smaller gains than what they could earn in silk factories. But I see not how this could be avoided, for were the schools to be suppressed the Children would still be made to commence the work as early in their own homes by their parents; and, as in those districts everyone nearly is a plaiter, instruction, though not so effective perhaps as in schools, would still be available.
>
> From the extreme poverty of the parents, and the scanty earnings of the Children they must be very poorly fed: but few of those I examined got meat more than once or twice a week.

Besides those who plaited for their living there were many who plaited part-time to make a little more money for specific goals. Some men and boys plaited after coming in from work in the fields to help the family finances, although they mostly plaited the simple twists. Gerald Massey, who worked at Tring Mill (see p. 70), turned to plaiting when he was out of work after the silk mill burned down. Lucy Luck (see p. 78) who worked at the same mill, felt that she had to make five yards of plait each night after work to help the kind widow with whom she lodged because her wages and the parish contribution were not sufficient to buy enough food to feed the family.

School log books illustrate the struggle between those trying to give the children what they considered to be a proper education far removed from that which the plaiting school provided, and what most parents wanted, which was for their children to produce as much plait as possible. Such parents saw education as something that could be forgone when there were more important things to be done like finishing plait for market day.

The problem of whether plaiting could be combined with education was faced by the committee of ladies managing Hitchin Girls' British School. Rules were laid down before it opened in 1819. Rule number nine read that, in addition to reading, writing, arithmetic and needlework, the committee could introduce additional employments such as knitting or straw-plaiting. It was obvious that the ladies did not wish to encourage straw-plaiting at the school because the rule went on to say that 'no rewards whatever be given to straw plaiting, it being rather tolerated as necessary than taught and encouraged as an advantage.'[11] However, not everyone agreed with the Hitchin ladies and, as has been mentioned, the Bishop of London was called as a witness to a Parliamentary committee in 1835. He had seen some plaiting schools and seemed to think that the introduction of 'work of industry' into National (Church of England) Schools might be no bad thing if properly managed.[12]

Most of the surviving school log books date from the 1860s and they show that many teachers did not like the effect that straw-plaiting had on the children's education and tried to discourage it, but they had to fight the opposition of parents and sometimes the interference of the local gentry and clergy. Potten End School provides a good example. The Honourable John Finch of Berkhamsted Castle set up a school at Potten End in 1856. He died in 1861 and his widow became solely responsible for the running of the new school.

The following entries in the school log book are all from 1864:

12 June	The Hon. Mrs Finch called as she passed the school in her carriage.
23 June	The Hon. Mrs Finch visited the school and heard First standard read.
27 June	Admitted two new scholars, several boys returned who have been previously at work.

30 June	Market day at Hemel Hempstead; many of the older children went with their parents to sell the plait.
4 July	Many of the older boys left for hay-making. Numbers very low, only 16.
13 July	The Hon. Mrs Finch visited the school.
18 July	Berkhamsted School Treat. Day holiday.
19 July	Sunday School Treat. Half holiday.
20 July	The Hon. Mrs Finch visited the school and procured a plaiting mistress.
20 July	Hemel Hempstead market day. Many scholars absent to sell their plait.
13 August	The Hon. Mrs Finch visited the school.
5 September	Re-opened school. Admitted fifteen children. The plaiting mistress commenced teaching at the school.
6 September	The Hon. Mrs Finch visited the school.
8 September	Half holiday. The children went to the castle [Berkhamsted Castle where the Hon. Mrs Finch lived] for their School Treat.[13]

The Honourable Mrs Finch, not the schoolmistress, decided that a part-time plaiting mistress be appointed in 1864 to lure the children away from the numerous plaiting schools in the area. She obviously meant well and helped the school in many ways, visiting frequently, hearing the children read, buying equipment and giving treats, but she made the life of the mistress difficult with her decision over plaiting. The plaiting mistresses were often absent and did not stay long in post, perhaps because they found it hard to adapt to the ways of an ordinary or 'reading' school. In January 1866 the teacher tried to reduce the time for plaiting because she thought that the girls needed more instruction in needlework. In April the plaiting mistress gave notice to quit, perhaps because of the reduction in hours, but a new plait mistress was appointed and came three days later. In June of that year the teacher wrote that some children were coming to school only to plait and another entry in the log book in July stated that 'the plaiters [are] very tiresome in the afternoon'. They probably did not take kindly to being required to do work other than plaiting.

At Great Wymondley National School it was noted in the log book in June 1868 that the children plaited in the afternoon until 3.30pm and then had one ordinary lesson. Another example of teaching plaiting in an ordinary school was at St Ippolyts in 1846

Figure 16. Girls plaiting at Titmore Green near Stevenage in front of a dilapidated cottage.

when a Miss Ross came in several times a week to teach plaiting.

At Boxmoor School, Hemel, straw-plaiting was taught even after the 1870 Education Act was brought in until a new master arrived in 1878 and stopped it. At Walsworth School on the outskirts of Hitchin it was noted that attendance went down when the price of provisions was high in 1853 because many parents kept their children at home to plait to earn more money. The managers decided to make the best of a bad job by hiring a girl to superintend plaiting within the school day.[14]

Even when the schools managed to exclude plaiting from their own classes they continually had to record that children were kept at home to plait to make money for

Figure 17. Pauper children with their band outside the workhouse in Bancroft, Hitchin, 1880. The girls all wear unbecoming straw bonnets.

clothes in good times or to take advantage of the rise in prices, and in hard times to help the family income. The children usually went with their parents to the plait markets, three of which at Hitchin, Hemel Hempstead and Tring were held on weekdays. Children were often withdrawn to go to plait schools and sometimes returned if the plait trade slackened. At Potten End in 1867 the children came more regularly 'on account of a decrease in the price of plait'. Conversely, in 1875 the log book of the Abbey School in St Albans records that 'as trade in the straw work keeps very active most of the girls are kept at home to help their mothers'.[15] It must have been very difficult for the children to make any progress when their attendance was so irregular and teachers must have despaired, especially after the method of 'Payment by Results' was introduced in 1862 as the financial grant for each school was calculated partly on the basis of attendance and partly on the children's progress, which they demonstrated by attaining certain standards in the year's tests.

The battle that the schools had with straw-plaiting did finally come to an end, partly because the Education Acts of 1870 and 1880 made attendance compulsory, but mainly because the industry declined and then collapsed in the face of foreign competition in the late 1870s. Until then straw-plaiting had provided a lifeline to many families in Hertfordshire but was a great hindrance to any meaningful education. Many of the plaiting families lived in towns like St Albans and Hitchin or in the villages where the accommodation was hardly any better. The poor state of most of the cottages has been described in Chapter 1 and the dilapidated state of the cottage at Titmore Green, near Stevenage, outside which the girls are plaiting illustrates this vividly.

On the whole the country children must have had cleaner air but reports of the Local Rural Sanitary Authorities in the second half of the nineteenth century contain accounts of ditches and streams, some along the sides of roads, full of sewage. In 1866 at Walsworth, near Hitchin, ten cottages drained directly into a stream and at Preston thirty-nine cottages had no water supply. In Pirton in 1861 William Dawson, a ten-year-old plaiter, was lucky to live in a cottage with three bedrooms instead of the more common two but eleven people had to sleep in the bedrooms. They shared a well with two other cottages and their waste drained into the moat ditch around the remains of the castle.[16] Such conditions led to the spread of diseases like typhoid and typhus in many villages. Housing conditions had not improved much by the end of the century but at least most of the children were in school until the age of eleven.

Endnotes

1. Dony, *The straw hat industry*, pp. 22–3.
2. Young, *Agriculture of Hertfordshire*, p. 223.
3. *Ibid.*, pp. 222–3.
4. Census, *Table of statistics*, 1851–81.
5. L. Grof, *Children of straw* (Buckingham, 1988), p. 67.
6. BPP 1864 (3414) XXII.1.
7. Grey, *Cottage life*, p. 70.
8. *Ibid.*, p. 74.
9. Potten End school log book, 1864–8.
10. BPP 1843 (431) XIV.1, evidence of Major Burns.
11. Hitchin girls' British schools papers, 1819–31, HALS, 67521-33.
12. BPP 1834 (572) IX.1, *Report from Select Committee on the State of Education*, p. 193.
13. Potten End school log book.
14. Quoted in N. Farris, *The Wymondleys* (Hertford, 1989), p. 296.
15. A. Goodman, *The story of the Abbey school: a nineteenth-century national school* (St Albans, 1991), p. 13.
16. Hitchin nuisance removal committee, 1866, HALS, BG/HIT/276.

Chapter 4

The silk industry

Beginnings

The Chinese learned to make silk nearly 3,000 years ago but they managed to keep the process a secret from the outside world for almost 2,000 years. Europe learned the secret in the sixth century AD when two Persian monks smuggled some silkworm eggs to the court of the Emperor Justinian in Constantinople. Gradually the skill of making silk spread to Italy, Spain and France. In these three countries the climate was warm enough for the silkworms to be cultivated to supply the raw material.

Silk-making reached England by the fifteenth century but the climate was too cold for the rearing of silkworms and so raw silk had to be imported. The industry expanded in the sixteenth and seventeenth centuries as skilled Protestant silk workers fled from religious persecution in France. Many of these immigrants settled in Spitalfields in London, while others moved to Colchester, Ipswich, Norwich, Maidstone and Sandwich. In the eighteenth century the industry expanded further as machines powered by water were introduced. Mills were built near fast-flowing streams in places such as Stockport and Macclesfield. Government legislation, meant to protect the workers of Spitalfields, had the unintended effect of making it more expensive to produce silk there, so further centres of production opened up in Braintree, Paisley, Leek, Derby and in south-west Hertfordshire.

There were two distinct processes in making silk: throwing and weaving. Throwing silk consisted of several stages. The raw silk would have been unwound from the silkworm cocoons and wound on to reels in its country of origin. When it arrived at the silk-throwing mill it had to be washed in white soap, graded and any knots in the fibres removed. The fibres, which were of various lengths, were then spun to produce one continuous thread. Several threads were combined or 'doubled' to make them stronger. Finally the threads were twisted again or 'thrown' in the opposite direction to

Figure 18. Tring silk mill in 1890 under the ownership of Lord Rothschild.

produce a strong elastic thread called organizine. The reels of organizine were then sent to the weaver. The silk-weaving looms resembled those used in cotton manufacture but heavier weights were needed to keep the warp threads taut. By the early nineteenth century the Jacquard machine, which used perforated card to produce patterns, was widely used and by the 1830s power looms were beginning to replace hand looms. However this was a slow process because it was, at first, difficult to produce fine silk cloth on looms powered by steam.

The silk industry comes to Hertfordshire

Hertfordshire had never had a flourishing textile industry but at the end of the eighteenth century the demand for silk and the expense of making it in London did lead to the setting up of silk-throwing and a few silk-weaving mills in the county. Attracted by relatively unpolluted rivers and by the proximity to London markets, enterprising manufacturers began to convert old unused corn mills, of which there were many, into silk-throwing mills and sometimes to build new mills.

The earliest silk mill in Hertfordshire was probably Rookery Mill at Watford which was built near the River Colne at the bottom of Deacon Hill, around 1770. In the late eighteenth century it was run by the Huguenot Paumier brothers and in the 1820s it passed to Thomas Rock Shute who ran it and another mill in Bushey. A directory of 1792 mentioned three silk mills in Watford and stated that 'silk throwing was the principal manufacture of the town'. The other two Watford mills were at Red Lion Yard and near Clarendon Road; they were probably powered by horses.

Other centres of the silk industry in the west of the county were Tring and Rickmansworth. William Kay, whose family had a silk business in Macclesfield, bought Tring Park Estate and built a mill in Brook Street in Tring in 1824, diverting streams into the mill pond to power his water wheel. Kay ran the mill for five years, handing it over to Messrs Evans of London in 1829. A twenty-five horse power engine was in place at the mill by 1840 and the workforce had expanded to around five hundred. The Batchworth Mill in Rickmansworth had several uses. In the late eighteenth century it was, surprisingly, a cotton mill run by a Mr Strutt, which had amongst its workers London children from the workhouse in St James, Piccadilly.[1] In the early nineteenth century it was a silk mill for a time until John Dickinson bought it and converted it into a paper mill (see Chapter 5). There was also a silk mill in Rickmansworth High Street.

By 1803 there was a silk mill in St Albans on the site of the old Abbey corn mill which was run by the Woollam family for most of the nineteenth century. A cotton mill making wicks for candles existed for ten to fifteen years in the mid-nineteenth century in Cotton Mill Lane, St Albans. There was even an attempt to set up a silk mill in the north of the county on the River Hiz. Joshua Ransom, a member of one of the influential Quaker families in Hitchin, ran Grove Mill in the town as a corn mill but around 1826 he turned it into a silk mill. He must have attracted local labour, for the annual reports from Hitchin Girls' British School from 1826 to 1829 show that thirteen girls, probably at the age of ten or under, left the school early to work in the silk mill.[2] Ransom may have tried silk-weaving as well because when an application was made for George Frost to join the Hitchin Boys' British School in 1829, his father's occupation was given as silk-weaver and his address was Grove Mill.[3] The experiments were not a success and Ransom had reverted to milling corn by about 1838.

A mill was set up at Hatfield Workhouse in 1818 using pauper children as the workforce, but it had closed by 1849. Redbourn Mill, unusually, opened as late as 1857 and seems to have been very successful, producing silk thread well into the twentieth century along with the Abbey Mill at St Albans. The silk produced would have been sold to silk-weaving mills, especially those near at hand in Braintree, and some may well have been sold to John Dickinson so that he could produce his paper shot through with silk thread to prevent fraud. There were a few attempts to weave silk in the county, both by individual weavers and by the mill owners, such as at the Evans's mill in Akeman Street, Tring, and, maybe, as mentioned, by Joshua Ransom at Hitchin, but these ventures were all unsuccessful.

Mill owners relied heavily on the labour of women and children under fifteen. This was partly to save money because they were paid less than men and partly because they were usually more nimble-fingered and could tie knots in the thin thread which had a tendency to break. The main reason may have been because they were a much more docile and easily controlled workforce. As a witness explained to the select committee of the House of Commons on child labour in 1833, mill owners preferred girls because boys were 'not sufficiently docile and do not submit so quietly to all the restrictions which are put upon them; the girls and young females are taken in preference to the other sex'.[4]

Child labour brought to Hertfordshire silk mills from outside the area

Mill owners complained that child labour was difficult to obtain in the areas where the mills were situated, blaming the large number of children engaged in straw-plaiting. To fill the gap, a tradition of recruiting children from workhouses in London and in the areas surrounding the mills began in the late eighteenth century. The parish of St Clement Dane in London in 1782 ordered that all pauper children above the age of six should be sent to the silk mills at Watford or elsewhere so that the parish might make a great saving. They would have the initial outlay of a premium to the owner of the mill and would have to provide the children's clothing but presumably they hoped to have no more responsibility for the children's welfare and no further expenditure. St James's, Piccadilly, sent two pauper children to be bound apprentices to Mr Strutt who ran Batchworth cotton mill at Rickmansworth. The St James's Guardians took their duties seriously and sent visitors to Strutt's mill in 1790 where they found that all was well. However, after a further visit in 1792, they reported that the food was inadequate and the hours very long, and that the children had been severely chastised for trifling offences. No more pauper children seem to have been sent from St James's.[5] The Batchworth cotton mill did not survive into the nineteenth century but now some of the silk mills in the county began to recruit pauper apprentices from the workhouses of London and elsewhere. St Martin-in-the-Fields sent twenty-four children to be apprenticed to Thomas Watson who had a mill in Watford High Street in 1796. The overseers of the poor made an unexpected visit in the same year to investigate a claim that the children were being ill-treated but concluded that the complaint was unfounded.[6] No more is heard of Watson's mill after he died in 1804 and the next contact that the overseers of St Martin-in-the-Fields had with Hertfordshire was when they sent three girls to be apprenticed to Charles Woollam of the Abbey Silk Mills, St Albans, in 1803. It is always said that the St Albans Mill began operating in 1804 but the vestry of St Margaret's, Westminster, was in correspondence with Woollam in January

1804 over a girl from its parish who was already at the mill and St Martin had three apprentices there in August 1803.[7] Some pauper children did not have to travel far to work at the mills. The Rickmansworth vestry sent children from the workhouse to the mill in Rickmansworth High Street which in 1807 was being run by William Harty who was also running Rookery Mill in Watford. When Harty died in 1826 Thomas Rock Shute took over both the Rickmansworth High Street and the Rookery mills.

Tring Mill, run from 1828 to 1879 by Evans and Company, was another mill that relied heavily on pauper apprentices. The minutes of the Aylesbury Board of Guardians show that pauper children had been sent to Tring Mill before 1838. In that year more children from Aylesbury were sent because the draconian order was given by the board that all people receiving relief from the Aylesbury Union who had children aged from eight to sixteen and capable of work should send them to Tring Mill.[8] The directive was probably not strictly enforced because David Evans who ran the mill liked to ensure that the pauper children sent to him were strong enough to do the work and in good health. He often had them on a month's trial and would send back any child who was a liability, for example, suffering from fits or weak ankles. The children he employed needed to be able to stand continuously for nearly twelve hours at a time.

Children's work in the mills

The young children recruited to work at the mills were usually employed in two processes: winding and cleaning. In winding, when the silk had been washed and graded, the skeins were placed on swifts, which were star-shaped skeleton reels, often with weights suspended from them to produce the correct tension. The children had to walk up and down continuously next to the unfenced machinery, watching for breaks in the threads and tying them up. They also had to replace the empty swifts with new ones while the machinery was still moving.

The second process in which children were involved was the cleaning of the silk. The thread was wound from one set of bobbins to another and in doing this any remaining bulges were removed, usually causing the thread to break. The thread was then tied up again. As young children had to concentrate on this work for up to twelve hours a day it is a wonder that not many accidents were reported. One fatal accident did occur in a Hertfordshire silk mill. The *Watford Observer* reported in February 1826 that an inquest was held into the death of a little girl called Ann Groom who got her clothes entangled in the unfenced machinery at the mill in Bushey and was crushed to death. The verdict was 'accidental death'. Employers did not seem to be much moved by the death of their employees and set up an association to resist legislation which would compel them to fence their machinery. Charles Dickens wrote an article on

Figure 19. A machine for winding silk, *c*.1840, showing the swifts that the children had to replace while the machinery was still running.

industrial accidents in his weekly magazine *Household Words* in 1856 referring to the employers' association as the 'association for the mangling of operatives'.[9]

Although the employers who ran the silk mills usually stated that they were looking for children of ten or eleven, children below ten were employed right up to the 1870s, as the census returns show. In 1861 sixteen boys and fifteen girls under the age of ten worked in Hertfordshire silk mills and in 1871 there were still twelve boys and ten girls of ten and under working in silk.

Much information can be gleaned from the reports to Parliament on silk mills, including those in Hertfordshire. William Rastrick and Daniel Fraser were called before a Parliamentary Select Committee in 1832 to give evidence on working conditions in the silk mills. The group of MPs asking the questions may have been mostly in favour of bringing working hours down to ten hours a day and so tried to expose the worst conditions by sometimes asking leading questions; also Rastrick had left Rookery Mill several years previously, but much of what he and Fraser described is borne out by evidence from other sources.

William Rastrick, called in and examined.[10]

Where do you reside?

At Watford.

What age are you?

Thirty-four.

Have you ever been in a silk mill?

Yes.

At what age did you go into one?

At 11 years of age.

Are there not many children that go at a much earlier period than that?

Yes, considerably younger.

How young have you known children go into silk-mills?

I have known three at 6; but very few at that age.

What time had you allowed for breakfast, for dinner and for tea?

Half an hour breakfast, half an hour dinner, but no tea time; at least at that time.

Was the mill worked at night?

No, not then.

Have you found that employment to be hard and laborious?

Yes, at times.

Was it fatiguing?

Yes.

Had you, or any of the hands an opportunity of going to an evening school, or of learning anything during that time?

No, it was too far from the town; a mile from the town.

Was there a Sunday-school in the town?

Yes, two or three.

Did those afford the hands, generally, the only opportunities they possessed of getting a little learning?

The only opportunity.

Were not the children very much disinclined to attend the Sunday-schools after having been thus employed during the week?

Yes, in a great many instances they would absent themselves from the school and ramble in the fields instead of going.

Were the children beaten up to their labour, so as to be compelled to do it?

Yes, at times.

What did you become afterwards?

At that time I worked at the spinning-mills; and from them I went to what are called the throwing-mills.

What age were you when you went to the throwing-mills?

About 11.

Were you a throwster?

Yes; I began learning the throwing department at that time.

Is not that an employment which requires very close attention?

Yes.

What hours did you labour there?

The same.

Has not the silk-throwing business to be performed in a standing position?

Yes, the whole of it.

Did not you find that to stand that length of time, to say nothing whatever about the employment itself, was very fatiguing?

Certainly.

Did it ever produce pain in your limbs?

Pain in my legs and my back.

Did you not find it very irksome to your feelings, to have to take those means of urging the children to the work?

Extremely so. I have been compelled to urge them on to work when I knew they could not bear it; but I was obliged to make them strain every nerve to do the work, and I can say I have been disgusted with myself and with my situation; I felt myself degraded, and reduced to the level of a slave-driver in such cases.

In the throwing department, you tie the broken ends, do you not?

Yes.

Is not that tying or piecing an employment that requires great activity?

Yes.

And therefore induces occasionally very much fatigue?

Yes; great fatigue occasionally.

Does not the material often cut the hands of those poor children?

Frequently; but some more than others; I have seen them stand at their work, with their hands cut, till the blood has been running down to the ends of their fingers.

When the work does not run well, is incessant activity demanded on their part?

Yes.

So that on the whole, the children are often exceedingly fatigued by that pursuit?
They must be.
And you have witnessed it?
Yes, I have.
And you have felt it yourself, when engaged in it?
Yes, I have felt it myself.
Is there a tendency in this system to become rather better, or is the work required more, and the labour altogether severer than it formerly was?
It is decidedly worse within the last four or five years than it used to be.
Is there more work required of the children than there used to be when you first knew the business?
Yes; on account of the competition which exists between masters; one undersells the other; consequently the master endeavours to get an equal quantity of work done for less money.

***Daniel Fraser*, called in and examined regarding a Watford silk mill in 1832.**

At Watford, in Hertfordshire, the mill is worked both day and night. In Hertfordshire, the children go at 6 in the morning and work till 7 at night and they have one hour and twenty minutes intermission. Then the night hands go on at 7, and work till 6 in the ensuing morning?
Yes ... In this mill, children were going in at 5 years of age, and those children have worked the usual hours. At this mill, if the children are not tall enough, stools are got for the infants; they have no Sunday-school, nor week-day evening school at this village; it is a little village where this mill is. I found that one of the children, Elizabeth Taylor, went to the mill at between 7 and 8-years-old, for 1s a week at first; she is now nearly 15-years-old, and has 3s 6d a week. There are instances there, where the wife is working during the night, and the husband working during the day; the amount of their wages is 20s a week; both their wages united, for working night and day.
Do you know whether the children are beaten up to their work there also?
Yes; they are regularly urged to their work by beating; they use canes in that mill to beat the children.

One statement by William Rastrick does seem inconsistent. He said that he had seen the little children with their hands cut and blood running down their fingers. If the children had worked with their hands in this condition it would have stained the silk thread and ruined the batch that was being produced. Otherwise Rastrick and Fraser's accounts are largely borne out by the testimony of two people who worked at Tring silk mill from the age of eight in the 1830s and 1850s.

Gerald Massey, the Chartist poet, was born in Tring to poor parents in 1828. His mother managed to save enough money to send him to a 'penny school' where he learnt to read but he soon had to contribute to the family finances and was sent to work in the Tring silk mill at the age of eight, receiving between 9d and 1s 3d a week for twelve hours' work a day. From his poems it is clear that he hated this life and rejoiced when the mill was destroyed by fire in 1836. He then turned to straw-plaiting and doing odd jobs for two elderly ladies who ran a school and took an interest in him. He later went to London to find a job instead of going back to the silk mill. As a notable artisan poet he reflected the feelings of oppression and hopelessness that some of the young workers, and sometimes their parents, had.

God shield poor little ones, where all
Must help to be bread bringers!
For once afoot , there's none too small
To ply their tiny fingers
(Extract from Gerald Massey's poem 'The Legend of little Pearl')

Pleasantly rings the Chime that calls to Bridal-hall or Kirk;
But Hell might gloatingly pull for the peal that wakes the babes to work!
'Come, little Children' the Mill-bell rings and drowsily they run,
Little old Men and Women, and human worms who have spun
The Life of Infancy into silk; and fed, Child, Mother and wife,
The Factory's smoke of torment, with the fuel of human life.
O weird white face, and weary bones, and whether they hurry or crawl,
You know them all by the Factory-stamp, they wear it one and all.
(Extract about life in Tring silk mill from Gerald Massey's poem 'Lady Laura')[11]

Lucy Luck was also born in Tring in 1848, twenty years after Gerald Massey, and had a similar experience of going into the silk mill at eight years of age. She told her story when she was an old lady but the events of her early years were still very vivid in her mind. Deserted by her drunkard husband, Lucy's mother had no option but to go into the workhouse with her four children. From there Lucy was sent to work in the Tring silk mills when she was not quite nine. She worked half the day at the mill and was supposed to have a half day's schooling under the terms of the 1844 Factory Act but this did not happen. She stayed at home in the afternoon to help the tailor with whom she had been lodged by the Guardians of the Poor. Like Massey, she remembered the sound of the mill bell ringing at 5.30am to summon the workforce to another long day at the mill. There were a few bright spots in Lucy's grim existence, all the result of kindness by her fellow-workers at the mill. One occasion was when she was turned out of her lodgings at short notice by the tailor, a drunkard like her father. Having no food, she was fed that day by the other mill workers. On another occasion, when she was very ill, the man in charge of the room where she worked was very considerate to her and hid her from the gaze of the overseer. She was then lodged with a kind old lady until the workhouse put her into service to save money. Here is her story in her own words:

> Well, I was not quite nine years old, when I was sent back to Tring with another girl to work in the silk-mills. Now I had got my mother and brothers to see sometimes, but this other poor girl had not got a living relation, so you can see she was worse off than I. We were sent to live with a Mr and Mrs D [the drunkard tailor and wife], who had a son about thirteen and a daughter about fifteen years of age...
>
> The first day I went to work I was so frightened by the noise of the work and so many things flying round, that I dared not pass the rooms where men only were working, but stood still and cried. But, however, I had to go, and was passed on to what was called the fourth room.
>
> I was too little to reach my work, and so had to have what was called a wooden horse to stand on. At that time children under eleven years of age were only supposed to work half-day, and go to school the other half. But I did not get many half-days at school, as Mr D was a tailor by trade, so I had to stop at home in the afternoon to help him with the work. But I have never been sorry for that, for I learned a lot by it. Neither was I eleven when I had to work all day at the mill.
>
> I can fancy children now at that age, having to work from six o'clock in the morning until six at night. Every morning at half-past five the bell would ring out, 'Come to the mill; come to the mill'. But still that would not have been so bad if we had a good home. But I was a drunkard's child, and the 'relieving officer' had found us a drunkard's home.

Then, after the tailor had turned the two girls out of his home:
It soon got spread around how we two were placed, and one and another gave us to eat and drink and we found that we had more than enough... At two o'clock on the Saturday, the time we were let off for the day, [we had] no home to go to. We wandered on with the rest of the mill hands, not knowing where we were going, but someone saw me, and told me I was to go and live with Mrs. H., a poor but respectable widow with three sons and a daughter. It was a far better home than I had been turned out of. Mrs. H. was a good woman. Now my money at the mill was only 2s 6d a week up to the time I left, and the Parish made this money up to 3s 6d and that was all anyone had for keeping us parish children, as we were called. How could anyone properly feed hungry children upon that? So, to add to it a little more, I had to make five yards of straw plait every night after I had done work at the silk-mill. But I had a very good time there. I don't ever remember one of them raising a hand to strike me. The Parish supplied my clothes; fairly good of the sort. I never remember having anything but cotton dresses, the old-fashioned lilac print capes like our dresses in the summer; and shawls in the winter; good strong petticoats and thick, nailed boots, both summer and winter; big coal-scuttle bonnets, with a piece of ribbon straight across them. I leave you to guess what we looked like. I can only remember having one plaything and that was a big doll that my sister left me when she died.

Soon after I had gone to Mrs. H. to live, I was taken so ill in church one Sunday, I did not know how to get home. I could not eat anything all day, and on Monday morning I could hear the bell, 'Come to the mill, come to the mill'. I did not know how to raise my head from the pillow that morning. I managed to get there somehow, and the master of my room was very good to me. He saw how ill I was, and knew how I was placed, and sent me to lie down at the top of the 'alley' as it was called. Now every day the overseer would go in each room, just before breakfast-time, dinner-time and evening. He would walk very slowly up the room, stop at every few steps, and then come back again and then would be gone. The master would tell me to stand to my work until he had gone. This went on for a week, and I lost three quarters during that time, but that poor widow had to be the loser of that money. How I went to work that week God only knows...

Now, I had been with Mrs H until I was thirteen years of age and 'Black Garner' as he was called (the relieving officer) came to see her one day and

> said, 'Fanny, I am going to take your girl away.' She said, 'Be ye, Mr J, and where be ye going to take her to?' He said, 'I am going to take her to St Albans, to service. It is about time she was off our hands. Get her ready by next week.' Yes! It was time I was off their hands, for I was costing them 9d a week besides clothing, and when I was obliged to go to him to ask for anything to wear, or to have my boots mended, he would treat me like a dog. A time or two, the boot-repairer could not mend them the same night, and he would lend me a pair. It did not matter about the fitting. Once he lent me a pair of button boots. I had never had such a thing on my foot before.[12]

Two young paper mill workers told the factory inspector in 1843 why they preferred working there to working in the silk mills.

> No. 208. *Sarah Sage*, aged 18. Examined 21 April 1843:
> Can't read or write. I think I have been here about a year. Rag-cutting. Was in the silk mill before, like this line the best; they beats you so there; they beat the little children shameful; my mother took me away; hadn't good health there; have had good health here.
>
> No. 210. *Daniel Haynes*, aged 15. Examined 21 April 1843:
> Can read and write. Attend a Sunday school. Been here a year and three months. Employed as a scratcher [one who uses a hackling machine with steel combs to scratch off the knots on the paper]. Before was at the silk mill; they beat me about a good deal there. Like it better here; come to work at six leave off at half past five.

By the 1840s punishments seem to have become less severe although *The Bucks Advertiser and Aylesbury News* reported on 17 April 1847 that two boys aged about sixteen named George Norman and Joseph Copcutt were brought before the Petty Sessions at Tring accused of running away from their employment at Tring silk mill. They had done this before and were each sentenced to one month's hard labour in Hertford Gaol. The girl apprentices were by now treated less harshly and the medical officers who reported in 1847 spoke of the punishment for refractory conduct as being limited to bread and water for two days, separation from friends and wearing inferior clothing on Sunday. Thomas Rock Shute, who owned Rookery Mill, claimed that he was humane and did not sanction the beating of children. He was known throughout the area as a hard taskmaster and had been cited, in an 1833 report to Parliament, as saying that, in extreme cases, punishment with a thin cane or even a slap on the face was justified. He also told his overseers not to flog a child so as to produce marks on the child's back.[13] As late as 1865 Elizabeth Gibson from Berkhamsted workhouse, who was working at Tring Mill, was subjected to violence, not in the workplace but when she got back to the lodging house, as a letter from the Berkhamsted Guardians reveals.[14] She had returned to find that she was given only bread and butter with no milk as her evening meal. When she complained to the master of the lodging house, he ordered her to bed. When she complained again he grabbed her and 'dragged her by her hair into the yard over stones and locked her in the wash house for about two hours'. To its credit, the Berkhamsted Board of Guardians protested at her treatment and said that the girls should be treated as apprentices, not as paupers. Their diet should sustain children who worked for ten and a half hours a day. The upshot was that the master and matron were dismissed.

Something is known about the diet of the apprentices at Tring Mill because in 1847 the medical officers from St Margaret's, Westminster, found the children eating peas, soup and bread while visiting the mill. They also made a note of the daily diet which was a little better than the food that the children had had back at the workhouse. One difference was that the supplies of food for apprentices were 'not limited in quantity'. One hopes that if the children asked for more, they got it.

Housing conditions

Not being well paid, the children only getting from about 1s to 3s 6d and adults up to 10s for a working week of up to sixty hours, silk workers mostly lived in the poorest part of town, often in squalid conditions. This is graphically illustrated in Inspector Clark's report to the General Board of Health on the state of housing in Watford in 1849.[15] It shows that silk workers, like papermakers, lived in some of the worst slum areas. In the 1851 census Sophia Brown, aged eleven, is shown working at the silk mill with her sixteen-year-old brother James. They lived in Red Lion Yard, one of the most notorious slum areas in Watford, with their widowed mother and her two other children. In the report of 1849 the yard was named as a fever locality after four cases of fever were reported at the Brown's, two proving fatal. The inspector said that 'the drainage is most defective and cannot be otherwise than extremely prejudicial to the health of the inhabitants residing in the cottages in the neighbourhood'. Sophia Brown must have

Figure 20. Church Street, Tring in the late nineteenth century showing the type of housing many silk workers lived in.

lived in constant fear of fever of one kind or another taking more of her family. Her ability to withstand the disease cannot have been helped by the fatigue brought on by the long hours that she had to work.

Like John Dickinson the papermaker, Thomas Rock Shute built cottages near his mill at Watford to let to his workers but, unlike those built by Dickinson, his cottages were not very desirable. He protested strongly when the local Board of Health condemned them for lacking ventilation, pure water and privy accommodation and said that they were damp. The *Watford Observer* reported in 1880 that the cottages were still in a deplorable condition.

The housing of many of the silk workers at Abbey Mills in St Albans was not much better than those at Watford. The *Hertfordshire Mercury* described some of the housing in St Albans in 1857, saying that there were piggeries next to cottages and that bone-boiling took place close to the homes producing noxious smells. In such insanitary conditions it is no wonder that typhus, spread by lice, was prevalent in the area. If the houses in Tring occupied by silk workers were like those of nearby towns described in the inspectors' reports of 1849–53, conditions were appalling , without a supply of pure water and with very unsatisfactory privies. It is no wonder that both typhus and typhoid, spread by polluted water, were an ever-present threat.

The 1851 census for Tring shows the sort of families from which the child mill workers came. Richard Dorset, a forty-nine-year-old agricultural worker, lived at New Mills, Tring, with his wife and four children. The three oldest, David, aged thirteen, Edwin, aged ten and Mary, aged eight, all worked as silk-cleansers. The youngest was a baby girl, a year old. There were five lodgers in the home: Rachael Bristow, a widow, her two girls aged thirteen and eleven, a nine-year-old boy and a one-year-old baby. Rachael was a needlewoman but the three older children were all silk-winders. The house in which the eleven lived must have been very crowded, but the practice of taking in lodgers to help with the family income was widespread and often a necessity for workers whose wages were so low.

There was one group of child workers who were a little better housed than most of the child workers living at home. These were the pauper apprentices working at Tring Mill. Tring still took children from St Margaret's, Westminster, until about 1867. Children from St George's, Hanover Square, St Marylebone and Berkhamsted workhouses were also still employed there in 1851.[16] There were fifty-four apprentices from London in Tring that year, four living in Brick End Lodge and the other fifty housed in a long, low building opposite the mill. Information on living conditions comes from the reports of the medical officers and other workhouse officials from London, Berkhamsted and Aylesbury who visited the mill and the lodging house. The children had a dining room in which to eat their meals and they had two hours of recreation in which they were expected to mend their clothes. There was some criticism of the bedrooms where girls slept two to a bed. The rooms were thought small and poorly ventilated and in 1849 the bedding was found to be scanty and not satisfactorily cleaned. Some of the iron bedsteads were broken. The matron excused this by blaming the children for breaking them and saying that they were left like that as a punishment. The man in charge of the mill at the time contradicted the matron and said that the state of the bedsteads and bedding would be remedied. In 1857 there was a less than satisfactory report by visitors from St Margaret's, Westminster. The house was felt to be overcrowded and a defective drain was causing bad smells. A watercourse was cleaned in 1859 and in 1860 the Board was pleased that the girls were in good health, that there was ample food and, at last, increased ventilation in the bedrooms.

It is interesting to contrast the accounts of Tring silk mill in *Osborne's London and Birmingham Railway Guide* of 1840 with the report of the visitors from St Margaret's Westminster in 1847.

Osborne's London and Birmingham Railway Guide of 1840 revealed some major problems:[17]

> The Silk Mill is in the occupancy and worked by David Evans & Co. of Cheapside, London; it was started by Mr. Kay, in 1825, since then it has been much increased in size, and is now capable of employing 500 pairs of hands, consisting of 40 men, 140 women, and 320 children. The number of hands in the mill is much less in summer than in winter, owing to the agricultural employment that is then afforded; this does not result from any superiority of wages, but from the natural desire to be in the open fields, and the aversion to monotonous and sedentary occupation, care and restraint. The superintendent gets a pound a week; the general run of the men's wages is between twelve and fifteen shillings a week; the average of the women's wages is five shillings and six-pence a week, and of children three shillings; the time of the latter is regulated by an Act of Parliament to ten hours a day, the adults work twelve.
>
> There is much difficulty in obtaining an inspection of the mill, in consequence of the jealousy resultant from competition; advantages having been taken by parties engaged in the trade, to convey a knowledge of the arrangements and mechanism to other manufacturers, an admission card from the proprietors is now required to be produced, prior to being shown through the rooms.
>
> By the side of the mill is the temporary residence of the proprietor, with a conservatory, and an extensive fish pool, the rather stagnant nature of which must give rise to much of pernicious effluvia; and considering that Tring is seldom or never without ague, and as malaria is found to result from pools of this character, several of which are in the vicinity, it is to be hoped that, ere long, the proprietors of these sources of pestilence will evince sufficient morality and intelligence to compel the removal of a nuisance so highly dangerous to all the neighbourhood; actually fatal to some, and deeply injurious to the lives and happiness of many innocent people.
>
> In the mill there are almost always persons whose haggard looks evince their lately having been afflicted with this terrible disease, evidently consequential to being employed in a building, through which there must, despite all precaution, be continually circulating a portion of the vapour from the pool beneath; the adults look bad enough; but the sight of the little

children who have lately suffered, with their wretched countenances, death-like colour, and tottering frames, cannot but make the heart of any humane person burn with the keenest anguish. The proprietors of the mill pay Mr. Dewsbury, surgeon, of Tring, £20 a year for inspecting the persons employed in the mill, to insure cleanliness and freedom from disease: after this evidence, we must not attribute the presence of the injurious marsh to a want of feeling in the proprietors, but rather a want of information on the subject.

The temperature of the mill is about 60°, and the people employed, though pallid enough, present a better aspect on the whole than those in the mills of Manchester, but still they are far from appearing to be a happy and healthy people; the children, in particular, appear doleful and dejected; some of them have a precocity of visage that is absolutely startling. They are taught to sing hymns as they work, and when a stranger comes, to affect a semblance of sanctity, and sing out with unusual energy; it would, perhaps, be a wise reform to do away with this schooling in hypocrisy; and peradventure it might be found that music of a livelier character would have a more stimulating and beneficial influence upon the nerves and general health of these poor innocents.

The medical officers of St Margaret's, Westminster, reported on their visit to Tring Mill in 1847 as follows: [18]

To the Board of Governors and Directors of the Poor of the parishes of St Margaret's with St John the Baptist, 13 May 1847.

The children for the most part appeared in good health, were neat and cleanly in their persons and appear very contented and happy. The domestic arrangements are also tolerably good and the kind and quantity of food are good and sufficient. The Dietary is as follows:

Bread daily	1 lb, eaten at meals during day
Breakfast	1 pint of milk
Dinner	Cooked meat 4 days a week
	Soup or rice and suet pudding 3 days a week
Supper	Cheese, about 3 ozs

The rate of sickness was very small, it is seldom that there are three children sick at one period and during 8 years only 1 death.

The only correction exercised in Case of Refractory conduct is a restriction to Bread and Water of no more than two days, with separation and compelling the offender to wear inferior clothing on the Sunday.

There was one peculiarity, on a careful examination, that needed investigation, it was that some of the children were afflicted with Bronchial and Glandular swelling on the first part of the Necks, in some of it slightly observable, and in 2 or 3 cases more prominently; pursuing our enquiries, we ascertained the Girls of the Neighbourhood were also afflicted with it, and the cause is referable to the Locality or the water, probably to both. Although the complaint is frequently referable to situation, and in no way dangerous in its consequences, we felt it necessary to see the medical attendant of the Establishment and learn from him, the result of his knowledge and experience of the ailment, and he informed us it was peculiar to the Neighbourhood, but that it seldom advanced beyond the condition we saw it, and rarely required medical treatment ...

The employment is not laborious, and can be in no way prejudicial to health. At present they labour 12 hours daily, Saturday excepted when they work only 9 hours; they rise at 5 o'clock in the Morning and commence their duties at half past 5, continuing until 7 o'clock in the Evening, having half an hour for Breakfast and 1 hour for Dinner and the Interval from 7 to 9 o'clock to repair their clothes and take recreation ...

We should strongly object to so lengthened a period of daily occupation, but we were informed by the Manager, that very shortly the new Factory Regulations would come into operation, whereby the children would be required to work 10 hours only, thereby affording them longer time both for instruction and recreation.

The children who are under 10 years of age, are employed for 7 hours only, daily, and have the opportunity of going to school for 3 hours. The Elder children, on the Sunday, go to the different Churches in the Neighbourhood, and, occasionally are taken on walks under the ... guidance of the matron and her assistant ...

The Work Rooms are spacious, well ventilated, light and cheerful, in the winter the temperature is regulated by Hot Air and usually ranges from 56 to 58 degrees.

The Sleeping Apartments are small but ill-ventilated but the

> accommodation is suitable and we returned to make some suggestion for the better ventilation of these apartments which the manager promised should be carried out.

Decline of the industry

The British silk industry suffered a great blow in 1860 when the Cobden Treaty was negotiated with France. Cotton, wool and silk manufactured goods from France were to be admitted to Britain free of duty but British cotton, wool and silk items were to incur a duty not exceeding 30 per cent when imported into France. This affected the demand for silk thread to be prepared for weaving and the industry went into decline. By 1880 all the Hertfordshire mills except Rookery Mill, Watford, Tring Mill, St Albans and Redbourn mills had closed. Rookery Mill closed in 1881 and was bought by the Watford Steam Laundry. David Evans and Company gave up running the Tring silk mill in 1878. Baron de Rothschild, who owned the land on which it stood, tried to continue working the mill in order to provide employment for people in the area but it ceased production in the 1890s. The Abbey Mill, St Albans and Redbourn mills continued production well into the twentieth century. The proportion of children under twelve employed in these mills decreased in the last decade of the nineteenth century but child employment did not die out altogether because of the part-time system of schooling, so there were some eleven-year-old children employed into the 1890s. In 1881 64 per cent of the workforce at Redbourn Mill was under fifteen.

Diversions and entertainment

Taking a last look at the children in the silk mills, it is possible to find a few lighter moments to leaven the hours of unremitting toil, although the Sabbatarians tried to quash even these.

William Rastrick in his evidence given in 1832 said that the children would rather ramble in the fields than go to Sunday school on their one full day off work. As mentioned before, the children from Aylesbury workhouse working in Tring were found to be playing hockey, pitch and bustle (probably a game played by throwing large buttons or counters rather like pitch and toss) and other games on a Sunday by a visitor from the Board of Guardians in 1839. Such innocent amusements on the Sabbath were frowned upon and the Board tried to put a stop to such behaviour by urging Mr Evans to start a Sunday school. Such schools usually lasted all day and left little time for play.

Rather more generous-spirited was the practice by the governors of the poor of St Margaret's, Westminster, of sending Christmas presents to their pauper apprentices at Tring. In 1851 the usual present of a pudding and some tea arrived but in 1854 money presents of 2s 6d were substituted by the governors.

Finally, four pauper apprentices from Tring Mill, who came originally from St Margaret's, Westminster, had a rare treat. They were on leave in London to visit relatives in 1851, the year of the Great Exhibition. The governors of the poor paid for the four to visit the Crystal Palace, accompanied by the schoolmistress from St Margaret's workhouse. The girls may well have sought out the stand displaying the wares of David Evans and Company of Tring Mill and they must have had so much to tell the other children when they arrived back in Tring.[19]

Endnotes

1. St James, Piccadilly, governors and directors of the poor minute book, 1786, City of Westminster Archives (hereafter CWA), D1871.
2. Hitchin British girls' school reports, 1828–9, HALS, 67528-67231.
3. Hitchin British boys' school, index of admissions, 1829, Hitchin British schools, Hitchin.
4. BPP 1833 (450) XX.1.
5. St James, Piccadilly, governors' minute book, 1792, CWA, D1874.
6. St Martin-in-the-Fields, church wardens and overseers' minute book, 1796, CWA, F2075, p. 145.
7. *Ibid.*, p. 362.
8. Aylesbury board of guardian minute books, 1838–9, Centre for Buckinghamshire Studies, Aylesbury, G/2/3.
9. E. Crooks, *The factory inspectors: a legacy of the industrial revolution* (Stroud, 2005), p. 21.
10. BPP 1833 (450) XX.1.
11. G. Massey, *My lyrical life, poems old and new* (London, 1889).
12. L. Luck, 'A little of my life', *London Mercury*, 13 (1925–6).
13. BPP 1833 (450) XX.1.
14. St Margaret's, Westminster, proceedings of the governors of the poor, 1865, CWA, E5230.
15. *Reports to the general board of health on the town of Watford, 1849–50*, by G.T Clark, HALS.
16. 1851 census for Brook Street, Tring.
17. *Osborne's London and Birmingham railway guide*, 1840, HALS holds a photocopy.
18. St Margaret's, Westminster, report of medical officers to the board of governors and directors of the poor, 1847, CWA, E5216.
19. *Ibid.*, June 1851.

Chapter 5

Papermaking

The establishment of papermaking in Hertfordshire

Papermaking in Hertfordshire employed significant numbers of children and young people in the nineteenth century; it is remarkable that it had established itself in such a predominantly agricultural county by the 1820s. The invention of printing in the fifteenth century gave an incentive to produce high quality white paper. The first known mill in England was set up by John Tate in 1490 in Hertford. Tate's mill was famous enough to be visited by Henry VII in 1498 and 1499 and to supply paper to Wynkyn de Worde who had worked with William Caxton, the first English printer, and who took over the business on his death. Tate's mill did not, however, survive his death in 1507. Papermaking was mentioned at Hatfield and Sopwell, St Albans in the seventeenth century[1] but was well-established in the county by the second half of the eighteenth century. Producers of hand-made paper were buying disused corn and fulling mills, especially in the west of the county along the Colne, Gade, Chess and Bulbourne rivers, in order to convert them to paper mills. They also made use of the clear water from the streams that filtered through the chalk in the Chiltern Hills and which did not discolour the paper. By the early nineteenth century there were also two paper mills on the Lea at Hatfield and Harpenden, and one at Standon on the River Rib. When wire mesh was needed for the paper machines, some wire workers who had produced mesh for the malting industry were able to transfer their skills to the paper industry.

In the 1780s Nicholas Robert, a Frenchman, invented a machine to make paper in a continuous length rather than in single sheets. He went into partnership with Pierre Didot. With the outbreak of the French Revolution the partners looked for a more favourable and peaceful environment in which to exploit their new machine. Didot's English brother-in-law persuaded the Fourdriniers, wealthy London stationers of Huguenot origin, to buy a share in the patent rights to Robert's machine and in 1803 the

Figure 21. Nash Mills, one of John Dickinson's paper mills.

Fourdriniers leased Frogmore Mill, Hemel Hempstead, in which to set it up. Frogmore Mill was near the Fourdriniers' existing paper mill at Two Waters. This was the point at which papermaking mills in west Hertfordshire began to employ significant numbers of people, including children. The paper mills were first worked by water power but by the 1820s steam power had been introduced. The owners of the mills took advantage of the Grand Junction (later Union) Canal, which had reached Hemel Hempstead in 1797, to bring in supplies and send out the finished products. The Fourdriniers laid out too much money, overreached themselves and went bankrupt in 1810. Frogmore Mill was sold to the Grand Union Canal Company, which leased it to John Dickinson, another ambitious London stationer. Dickinson had seen the demand for paper increase in the early part of the century and acted as a middleman supplying paper to the East India Company. He decided to make paper himself so, with his partner George Longman of the London publishing family, he bought the Apsley and Nash Mills near Hemel Hempstead in 1810. Dickinson made improvements to Robert's machine and developed other inventions such as an improved cartridge paper and a machine to extract water during the production process. He was to become by far the most important figure in Hertfordshire papermaking and was, when judged by the standard of the time, generally an enlightened employer. By the 1820s, having introduced steam power to drive his machinery, he made full use of the Grand Junction Canal to bring in coal and other supplies and to transport the finished paper to London. In 1818 Dickinson took over a small paper mill at Batchworth, Rickmansworth, solely to produce pulp, or half-stuff as it was called in the industry, and he also built two further mills at Home Park, Abbots Langley in 1825 and Croxley, Rickmansworth in 1830.[2]

After the introduction of the Penny Post in 1840, Dickinson seized the opportunity to exploit the large market for envelopes, stationery and, later, postcards that he realised would open up. He cashed in on the Victorian fascination with symbols of mourning by offering about seventy-four different styles of mourning envelope. Dickinson also produced paper for cartridges for the army and paper containing silk thread, difficult to copy, which helped to prevent fraud. The government quickly took up this last idea and bought such paper in large quantities. As Dickinson's company expanded he needed more workers and looked for local children and young people as well as adults to swell his workforce. The children made up the numbers and cost less than adult workers. From the statistical tables issued after the census returns we can make some estimate of the numbers involved. The statistical returns issued after the first four censuses from 1801 to 1831 gave some indication of occupation but did not break down the population by age. The 1841 census was the first one to do so. This census broke the table of occupations down into people under and over twenty years of age. According to the tables approximately thirty boys and twenty-nine girls under twenty were employed in Hertfordshire in papermaking. The figures for 1851 to 1871 gave a finer breakdown, recording people working in papermaking who were between five and ten years of age and those between ten and fifteen.

Census year	Girls under 10	Girls 10–15	Boys under 10	Boys 10–15
1851	0	15	9	72
1861	1	15	10	72
1871	1	6	0	95

These census figures do not seem to take into account the 250 boys making envelopes at Apsley Mill mentioned by John Evans, a managing partner of Dickinson's, in his evidence to a factory inspector in 1867.[3] Figures from Dickinson's mills in 1881 list 145 boys, age not specified, but presumably under fifteen, and 85 girls working in its various mills. These figures were influenced by fluctuations in trade and the changes in legislation concerning the regulation of workplaces and education.

Some of the small mills making paper by hand did not prosper and began closing from the 1820s onwards. A few mills which modernised by installing the latest machines, such as Sarratt, Mill End, Loudwater, Solesbridge and Scots Bridge, Rickmansworth, Hamper in Watford and Standon on the Rib, were still working in 1851, but many had closed or been converted to other uses by the beginning of the twentieth century.

Children's work in the paper mills

To understand what work children did in the paper mills, it is necessary to describe the basic process of papermaking. It began with the collection, cleaning and cutting of rags into squares which were then soaked in an alkaline solution. The squares were beaten by mechanical paddles which were at first driven by water power and later by steam. This produced 'half-stuff', a kind of pulp. Impurities had to be removed from this pulp before it was ready for use. When paper was made by hand the stuff was poured into moulding frames called deckles, producing single sheets which had to be dried by being placed between felts. When a machine was used it formed the paper from the stuff on a wire frame over rollers, water power being used at first and then steam from the 1820s. The resulting paper was at first hung out to dry but Dickinson invented a machine to dry paper on the roller. The paper was then glazed between copper and zinc plates and coated with alum and animal size to prevent it from blurring and absorbing the ink.

Children were employed in various processes, starting with the rag rooms. Girls were usually employed alongside women to sort and cut up the rags, an essential part of the raw material used in papermaking during much of the nineteenth century. Boys were sometimes to be found in the rag rooms as well. Preparing the rags would usually mean ripping seams carefully so that the sewing thread was detached and could be ground up easily by a later process and did not spoil the pulp. Buttons, belts and buckles also had to be removed and then the rags were sorted into different types of cloths and colours before being cut into three- or four-inch squares with scythe blades fixed upright to the work benches. As much dirt as possible was removed, but inevitably the air was full of dust and fibres.

The hours of work of the children in the rag rooms were usually from 6am to about 5pm on weekdays and 3pm on Saturdays. The hours were shorter in winter because no candles were allowed in the rag rooms to guard against the risk of fire so work finished when daylight faded. In the 1840s the children in the rag rooms earned from four to six shillings a week in summer. Later gaslight was introduced meaning the children worked longer in winter and earned a little more.[4]

Boys were employed in watching the pulp-grinding engine and in picking out smuts, known as 'black spots', and other impurities from the stuff being ground down. They worked twenty-four hours on and twenty-four hours off, in order to ensure that there was a constant supply of pulp for the papermaking machines. An incentive to keep the boys focused on their work was the opportunity given to them in Dickinson's mills to make a little extra money on top of their wages. Each boy had a board marked in nine-and-a-half-inch squares. It is not known how big the board was but each board filled with 'black spots' picked out of the pulp earned them two pence to be added to their wages.[5]

Girls were often employed in separating the dried paper and glazing it to give a good surface for writing or printing. They preferred this work because, although it sometimes involved heavy lifting, it was a much cleaner atmosphere than in the rag rooms. After the 1840s girls and boys were employed in some mills in making envelopes and other stationery and a few boys helped with paper-staining. Others had to break up the esparto grass which was imported from the middle of the century to replace rags in making certain types of paper.

The reports to Parliament by factory inspectors cast light on working practices and contain interviews with individual children working in Hertfordshire paper mills. Some employers questioned the way in which the evidence was collected and thought that the reports gave a view of conditions biased against mill owners and in favour of those wishing to reduce working hours. However, the children's views are unrivalled in giving a glimpse of their working lives. Even without a list of the questions asked by the inspectors, it is easy to see from the children's replies that these were entirely factual.

Major Burns, a factory inspector, reported on working conditions in the paper mills of Kent, Buckinghamshire and Hertfordshire in 1843 and interviewed some of the children working at various mills in the county. These are his reports of these interviews.[6]

MR. MAGNAY, Mill End Mill [the owner and name of each mill are identified]

No. 202. *Joseph Avery*, aged 17. Examined April 21

Can read and write; used to attend Sunday school. Been here eight months, employed laying paper [laying it as sheets as the paper dropped from the cutting machine], sit down to work. Come to work at 4 o'clock most mornings, leave off sometimes at seven, and sometimes at eight. Eat my meal while at work; find it difficult when we have thin paper [because they had to keep attending to the machine without a break]; plenty of victuals. It isn't hard work you know but makes us sleepy; don't tire very much. Was three weeks ill before Christmas; don't know what it came from, whether being in the hot machine house or not; have good health now. Regular wages 6s a week; when work till 12 at night have 6d extra, not often do that. No beating allowed, well used.

(signed) JOSEPH AVERY

No. 203. *Benjamin Bryant*, aged 14. Examined April 21

Can read and write a little; don't attend any school. Been here rather better [longer] than a year. Hours of work and [nature of] work same as last boy. Forced to get a mouthful how we can, to eat our victuals. Work not hard, but tedious; never been ill since I've worked here. Hired by Mr. Magnay, paid by Mr. Howard the foreman; regular wages 6s 6d a week; paid for extra work, half a day five hours; not often work that way; work draws us to sleep, don't feel tired except [when] we work very late; well used. My father works here; receive my own wages.

(signed) BENJAMIN BRYANT

No. 204. *Joshua Avery*, aged 13. Examined April 21

Can read and write; attend school every evening except Saturday. Been here about nine months; employed at the scratcher [sort of rake by which the ground-up rags are cleared of pieces of straw, etc.] put in the stuff. Come to work at six, leave off about half past five; half an hour for breakfast, one hour dinner; go home to meals. My father works here; stand at work; not very hard, except we have a good deal of stuff. Sometimes, not very often, when they want the stuff, work till nine. Paid extra for that. Don't feel tired when leave off at five, do when I sit up till nine.

Haven't been ill since I've been here. Regular wages 10d a day. Hired and paid as last boy; well used.

(signed) JOSHUA AVERY

No. 205. *Ann Gibson*, aged 13. Examined April 21

Can read very well can't write. Attend Sunday school. Been here about a twelve month. Rag-cutting. Been employed straw-plaiting. Like this work best because it is not keeping your eyes on it. Come to work at eight and leave off at five. An hour for dinner, go home to it, Father and mother work here. The work is not very hard, does not tire me; stand at work. When I first came the dust used to make my head ache, but it don't now. Paid by weight. Earn about 5s or 6s a week. Hired by Mr. Magnay, paid by him sometimes, and sometimes by Mr. Hayward. Receive my own wages. Well treated. Did not like the situation, but do now.

ANN GIBSON Her mark

COMMON MOOR MILL. Messrs. Dickinson and Longman

No. 212. *Emma Davis,* aged 14. Examined April 22

Can read, but can't write much. Attend Sunday-school. Picking paper. Been here very near three years. Sit at work. Come to work at nine. No set time for leaving off; sometimes after dinner, or at three, the latest is about five. Work not very hard, does not tire nor hurt my health. Earn sometimes 4s or 5s a week. Hired by Mr. Alcock, paid by Mr. Rocket, another foreman who looks after the women. My father works here. Receive my own wages. Kindly used. Like the place very well, Take our time at dinner, eat it here; places for warming it, comfortable, and warm room in winter, not very hot in summer.

(signed) EMMA DAVIS

No. 214. *Eliza Kempster,* aged 13. Examined April 22

Can read, not write. Attend Sunday school. Been here nearly two years off and on. Employed in the dusting-room; we have to shake up the stuff after it comes out of the duster. Stand at work. Come to work at eight, go home at four; an hour for dinner, go home or eat it here as we like. My father, sister, and brother works here. The work ain't very hard, does not tire; never staid at home from illness. Where we work it is very cold in winter, but there is a fire in the next room, and the woman we works with tells us to go and warm ourselves when we are cold. Regular pay 3s a week. Receive my own pay; the woman we works with takes it from Mr. Alcock, and then she pays us. The woman is very kind. Plenty of good food.

ELIZA KEMPSTER her mark

No. 215. *David Kempster,* aged 12. Examined April 22

Can read and write. Go to school three days a week at Watford. Been here two years. Picks the blacks out of the stuff in the engine [the pulp-grinding engine]. Come to work at seven one morning and go away at seven next morning. Have four hours sleep in that time. Off work 24 hours, half-an-hour for breakfast, one hour and a half for dinner, and one hour for tea allowed; eat meals at the mills. Sometimes we can sit down, not often work very hard, feel tired when we go home in the morning. Never been ill, or staid away from work. Regular wages 3s a week; my father takes it; paid by Mr. Alcock, Well used, no beating. Plenty of good victuals.

(signed) DAVID KEMPSTER

No. 216. *Joseph Davis*, aged 10. Examined April 22

Can read and write. Attend school three days a week. Been here four months. Work hours, meals, hiring, etc, same as last boy. Sometimes feel tired. Never staid away from bad health. Get five hours sleep. Very cold in winter; a fire near us, where we can go to warm ourselves.

(signed) JOSEPH DAVIS

HAMPER MILL, Mr. Smith

No. 217. *Eli Crutchfield*, aged 10. Examined April 22

Can read and write. Attend the British school; my brother and me takes turn slice drawing [removing damp sheets of paper from between the felts where they had been pressed] one goes to school while the other works. Employed drawing slice. Come to work at half-past five, leave off at six mostly, sometimes sooner sometimes later, never later than seven. Sit at work. Half an hour each for dinner and breakfast. Go home to meals. Work ain't hard, does not tire much. Sometimes have not very good health, not from the work; sometimes a pain in the side, and sometimes headache. Where we work is very cold in the coldest weather. Earn sometimes 4d a day; father receives it. My brother earns the same. Plenty of good food. No beating allowed. Well treated.

(signed) ELI CRUTCHFIELD

No. 218, *Ann Atkins*, aged 13. Examined April 22

Can read and write. Attend Sunday school. Been here a year last November. Sometimes employed glazing paper, and sometimes in rag-house, like the first best. Sometimes, not very often, come to work before breakfast. Six o'clock is the right time. Leave off at five, and three on Saturdays. An hour for dinner, go home. Father and mother work here. Work isn't very hard, does not tire or hurt my health; once I cut my thumb, staid away about two months. Earn about 4s or 5s a week in rag-house, about the same in glazing.

Sometimes sit and sometimes stand. Where we work, comfortable and warm in winter. Hired and paid by Mr. Smith. Well used; no abuse or beating at all. Like the place.

(signed) ANN ATKINS

APSLEY MILL, Messrs. Dickinson and Longman

No. 228. *Thomas Child*, aged 13. Examined April 23

Can read very fair. Can write a little. Attend Nash Mill Sunday [school], Mr. Longman's. Been here a month. Employed in picking out knots and blacks from pulp engine. Come to work at seven, leave next morning at seven, then 24 hours off work; one hour for breakfast, one hour for dinner, one hour for tea, eat meals in the cabin close to the engine-room. Get about four hours' sleep, sometimes five. Sometimes break alum for an hour and a quarter; that's the hardest work, the other parts of the work is not hard because we can sit just on the side of the engine, and see the blacks. Feel tired after breaking the alum, not otherwise. Every time we work, we are also partly employed stacking the stuff [which] wets my feet and trousers, when done we can go up to the cabin and dry them. Have got a cold these two or three days, don't know how I caught it. When I work four journeys [days' work] in the week, get 4s and when three, 2s 6d. Hired and paid by Mr. Ratheney, receive my own pay, give it to my mother. Kindly used, never beaten. Plenty to eat and good victuals; there is a large family of us though, there is seven of us.

(signed) THOMAS CHILD

No. 229. *Joseph Woodell*, aged 14. Examined April 23

Can read and write. Attend Mr. Longman's Sunday school at Nash Mill. Been here four years. Work, hours, meals, hiring and paying, the same as last boy. Get four or five hours' sleep always. Don't feel it very cold in winter now that I'm used to it, it feels colder to them as first comes on, can go and warm ourselves at the cabin fire. Isn't very hard work at all, doesn't tire, never makes me feel never right bad [*sic*]. Never was beaten in my life to hurt me since I came here, have a very good master. Receive my own wages, they are the same as Child's, give it to my mother. Never had no holidays.

(signed) JOSEPH WOODELL

Major Burns and his assistant inspectors then summarised the children's reports. As these contained many examples taken from the counties other than Hertfordshire, most of the summaries have no relevance to this book. They did, however, highlight the problem of dusty, dirty rags, especially those coming from London. They concluded that 'the operations of picking, parting, and glazing paper are very cleanly and healthy. Rag-cutting is of all the work in paper mills by far the most unpleasant, and one would think from the thick atmosphere breathed must be in the extreme unhealthy, yet it really is not so, those working at it looking on the whole as robust and healthy.' They also commented favourably on Longman's school at Nash End, noting that it was a Sunday school, attended by sixty children and young people but not confined to those in the paper mill. Holidays were very short and very rare. They approved of piece work as the 'natural encouragement held out for work ... It is self-evident that the more they do the more they can earn.'

While Major Burns did find the atmosphere of the rag room oppressive, he seemed to accept the verdict of the employers and some doctors that it was not harmful. The children themselves seemed to have been similarly acquiescent but in their case they needed the work and the wages to survive and therefore had little choice in the matter. It had been widely reported from observations of conditions in the northern textile mills that some children were sick and had headaches when first exposed to the dusty polluted atmosphere. It was said that they had so-called 'mill fever'. From the extracts above it seems that Ann Gibson and Eli Crutchfield may have had symptoms of 'mill fever' caused by the dusty atmosphere.

It is difficult to judge how open the children were in their answers, although one boy plainly said that his master could be spiteful. They needed jobs to help with family finances and they felt that, in comparison with other employment such as working in the silk mills, conditions were reasonable so they were resigned to their lot in life. They did get tired and cold and worked very long hours, sometimes doing compulsory overtime when an order needed to be completed quickly. For example, a ship bound for Australia full of Dickinson's paper sank in 1870 and all the workers at the mills put in long hours every day and every other night to replace the lost paper.[7] However, all the children interviewed felt that they were well-treated and gave instances such as being allowed to warm themselves at the fire when they got very cold. Thomas Child could dry his feet and trousers when he got wet stacking stuff. Even the boys who worked twenty-four hours on and twenty-four off were grateful that they were allowed to take it in turns to snatch a few hours sleep in the night; this gratitude for small mercies perhaps shows the weakness of their position. Several of them made a point of saying that they were not beaten as the children were in the silk mills. Corporal punishment seems to have been discouraged and the children

Figure 22. Loudwater Mill, where the owner occasionally hit the children but was sometimes sorry for it afterwards.

counted themselves lucky that there was some consideration for their welfare. The only employer who did not eschew corporal punishment was Mr Plaistow of Loudwater Mill, Rickmansworth. One boy, George Gibson, who worked at the mill said, 'When in fault master sometimes hits the children or gives them a slap on the face; does not hurt very much, a stroke on the back with a cord, or strike often; sometimes he hits a hardish blow, and is sorry for it after'. At the same mill another boy said, 'Sometimes when master is spiteful he do give [*sic*] us a hard knock, not very often'.

Major Burns asked about the children's education. Of the twelve children interviewed, all except two could sign their names and all the children said they could read, although four said they could write only a little. All except Benjamin Bryant had been to some sort of school. The Sunday school mentioned was probably that started by Mr Longman for the mill children. John Dickinson built a school at Nash Mills in 1847 and his daughter Harriet began a school for the village girls of Nash Mills around 1855, while her husband John Evans founded a school for boys at Frogmore End. Some families must have had a little spare money or have made sacrifices, not only losing the boys' earnings but also having to find the school fees because two boys attended school three days a week and two brothers took turn and turn about at school and at work. Thirteen-year-old Joshua Avery seemed determined to get an education. He attended evening school every day except Saturday even though he sometimes had to work until 9pm.

Inspectors reported again on the Hertfordshire paper mills in 1867. John Evans, Dickinson's son-in-law in charge of the mills, gave evidence. Some things had changed for the better such as the fact that no boys at his mills were employed under the age of ten and a half. This was not so at all the mills. Mr Austin of Solebridge Mill, Rickmansworth, was prosecuted in 1879 for employing a boy whom he knew to be under ten, the legal age at which he could commence work. It was Austin's word against that of the boy who maintained that he had told Mr Austin he was nine going on ten. It is interesting that birth certificates were not mentioned in the court case as a way of verifying the boy's age but the magistrates believed the boy and Austin was fined £7 17s 6d.[8]

Evans still employed boys of eleven to work twenty-four hours on and twenty-four hours off in 1867 but he said that most of the boys worked a twelve-hour day making envelopes and were sent to school some of the time, as the 1844 Factory Act laid down. Their wages did not seem to have risen appreciably in the twenty odd years since the children were last interviewed. Not many accidents were reported at the paper mills but Evans's story, below, of the death of a boy at Nash Mills is shocking even though it was claimed that he was doing something he had been forbidden to do. The question of why no supervisor was about at the time was not asked.

Report on Nash Mills, 1864[9]

The inspector reporting on conditions in Nash Mills said that in September 1864 the lads under eighteen years of age employed at Nash Mills were eighteen in number, only three being under thirteen; the youngest was aged eleven years and two months.

> *Mr John Evans:* I am managing partner in the firm of Messrs Dickinson and Co. paper manufacturers. We have a number of mills all along the stream from Two Waters to Rickmansworth; the one that you have already seen supplies four others with the 'half stuff' or fibre to be made into paper. At this mill and the others where the paper is made, the manufacture is continuous from 12 on Sunday night with water power, and from 6am on Monday with steam power day and night until Saturday night. I believe it is true that some boys have been met coming from our mills early on Sunday morning; that,

however, would be an extremely rare occurrence. They work in journeys [days] 24 hours on and 24 off. The boys who work in that way are chiefly employed in picking any foreign matter out of the half stuff as it is being ground to pulp in the rag engines; they take it in turns to lie down during the night, and after a certain time the picking ceases, that it to say, the time comes, when the pulp in the engine has been completely picked, but still requires further grinding; then the boy has nothing to do. Our rule is to take none under ten-and-a-half years of age, and from that up to 13 and 14. We have schools, and compel one group of boys each day to attend them. We probably employ more than the usual proportion of boys, taking all our mills together; for at one there are 150 or so folding envelopes; theirs is only day work, 6 to 6, with two hours for meal times, and they leave at 2pm on Saturday.

Boys can earn from 3s to 7s or 8s a week with us. We also employ boys at the cutting machines to 'catch' the paper; but as those machines are separate from the machine that makes the paper, they do not work day and night. The paper as it is made is 'reeled' off, and taken to another machine to be cut. A cutting machine can cut in the day as much as is reeled off in a day and night.

We do not scrape our strainers, as the paper is being made, and therefore do not employ boys for that purpose. We have had serious accidents, but not from cogwheels catching parts of dress. A short time ago one of our lads was killed in trying to put on a strap to set some machinery going. It was no part of his work: indeed, he had no business to be in the place at all. It is not known how it happened, for it was just after breakfast, and no one was there. I do not think that any system like that of the factory half-timers working by relays could answer in a sparse country population. We try as far as we can to make a certain proficiency in the elements of education a preliminary to employment; some general scheme of that kind might be made to work.

Mr. Peacock (foreman): The boys at our cutting machines very rarely exceed their ordinary hours, six to six; they certainly do not make two hours overtime in a week, taking the whole year round, and that would not happen continuously night after night for a fortnight or a month, but only for a night or two now and then. We have as many cutting machines as we have papermaking machines, and can cut two sheets at once (that is to say, can have the paper of two reels passed under the knives of our machine at the same time); of some kinds of paper we can cut more than two at once.

> The hours of the women who sort the paper are from 9am to 5pm with an hour for dinner; they are on piecework, and never stay for more than an hour beyond their usual time; only one of them is under 18. Our stoppages in the ordinary course for cleaning felts and wires, changing sorts, etc are usually arranged so as to take place at breakfast time; I should say that our machines are shut down every morning from 8.30 to 11, or thereabouts.
>
> *Samuel Lendon:* Am 13; have been here four months; I pick [blacks] at the engines; begin work at 6am and go on till 6 the next morning; at 10pm I always lie down and go to sleep till 2am; when I am asleep, that other boy is on.
>
> *Henry Lane:* Am 11 years 10 months old; began here last July 12 months; I go on till 2am tomorrow morning; then I shall lay down from 2 to 6. I shall get half an hour's sleep before that, at about 11pm tonight. I came on at 6 this morning; when I am asleep the other boy is on.

A note was added by the inspector: 'both these boys and one or two others whom I asked had been to school and could read'.

Conditions at Apsley Mill, 1866

Reporting on Apsley Mill the inspector wrote the following:

> Nearly 250 lads from the age of 11 upwards are employed here; some in the manufacture of paper but the majority in making envelopes. I examined more than a dozen boys between the ages of 12 and 17: most of them could read without much difficulty a verse of a hymn, which consisted of words of one syllable, and could answer simple questions of Bible history. None had learned any geography, and few any cyphering [simple arithmetic] beyond addition and the multiplication table. The words enmity, continue, atoning were read correctly by three or four only. The words image, inspired, coward, captive, by six or seven. By a rule of the establishment, all the younger ones were compelled to attend Sunday school, and books of such attendance were kept by the respective masters, and regularly forwarded to the resident foreman. Any boy who had not been to Sunday school had to go to the day

school at Nash Mill for the greater part of one day in the following week.

Several of them attended an evening school which was held on three or four nights in the week during the winter months. A very intelligent lad aged 17, whose name I omitted to ask, a layer at the cutting machine, told me that he had worked in the mill for seven years, and had got all his learning from evening school.

The foreman stated to me that he had for some years been strict about admitting none before they were at the least 10 years old, but still some who were younger now and then obtained admission by the misrepresentation of their parents.

Frederick Rolfe: Am 12; have been here 8 months; used to cut straw for straw-plaiting before that; began that at seven years old. Have never been to any school but Sunday school since that; know something about Daniel and lions; not about Elijah.

H. Atkins: Am 12; have been here for two years; went to a day school for about two months; don't know who Judas Iscariot was; Jesus Christ is everybody. [The inspector says that Atkins] reads badly.

Thomas Sear: Shall be 12 in the month before Christmas; don't know what month that is nor what month Christmas is in; can't tell you the first month of the year, nor what month this is. Have been here three parts of a year; have not been to any day school for four years: worked in the fields before I came here. [The inspector says that Sear] reads letter by letter.

Girls also made envelopes and there were sixty-six so employed in Apsley Mill in 1881. Wages for the girls were very low even towards the end of the century; an anonymous poem in the *Hemel Hempstead Gazette* in February 1897 stated that the girls received three-quarters of a penny for a thousand envelopes and begged for one penny a thousand to make a living wage.[10]

Housing

Some of the mill children were lucky enough to live in cottages built by John Dickinson for his employees near to his mills as there was little housing in the vicinity. He began building substantial cottages in 1825, letting them to his workers at a rent of 2s 6d a

Figure 23. The envelope printing room staff at Dickinson's Apsley Mill, 1895.

week. After his death in 1869 the firm carried on the tradition of providing accommodation for its workers by building fifty cottages around what became known as Dickinson Square in 1890.

Some of the children who worked at Dickinson's mills would have lived in these cottages in reasonable conditions but those who lived in Watford and in other cottages in Hemel Hempstead had to endure much harsher conditions. The report to the General Board of Health written by George Clark in 1849 painted a damning picture of Watford as a town that had grown too rapidly, with the erection of shoddy buildings leading to a proliferation of unsavoury courts, many of which were named as fever localities in the report. Watford also had six slaughterhouses and 'very numerous pigsties' which, in the words of the report, 'were most offensive'. In 1851 Farthing Lane was home to two nineteen-year-old paper mill workers, Caroline Culverhouse and Joseph Davis. The 1849 report on Watford said that Farthing Lane 'was without drainage save a few open gutters and had all open cesspools and ill-conditioned privies'. Twelve-year-old James Groom, who also worked at the paper mill, lived in Meeting Alley where seventy-four people were crowded into thirteen tiny cottages.[11]

Hemel Hempstead was not much better than Watford and those not lucky enough to occupy a Dickinson cottage usually had to live in squalid conditions. In 1851 William Larkin aged nine and Job Tomlin aged ten, mill workers, lived at Two Waters village which was liable to flooding because of the way the mill impeded the flow of water. According to the report sent to the General Board of Health in 1853, sometimes the

Figure 24. Cottages built by John Dickinson for his workers.

sewage built up in the river because of obstructions as well. Thomas Child mentioned his large family in his interview with Major Burns in 1843. The following extract from the 1841 census for Frogmore End shows that there were eleven people living in Thomas's house, including three who may have been relatives or lodgers. Most such houses had only two bedrooms, rarely three, and Thomas Child's house is typical of the overcrowded state in which many of the labouring classes lived.

Frogmore End	Jonathan Child	42	Labourer
	Elinor Child	40	
	Alan Green	22	
	Charles Green	25	Labourer
	John Child	17	Labourer
	Mary Child	15	
	George Child	14	
	Thomas Child	6	
	William Child	3	
	Elinor Child	1	
	Sarah Hosier	72	

Improvements towards the end of the century

A series of Factory Acts improved the lot of the children, notably the 1844 Factory Act that required children in factories and mills to attend school for about three hours a day. The 1867 Act and its extension brought paper mills under the control of all previous factory legislation. The 1874 Act raised the age below which children could not work in factories to ten and that of 1878 consolidated all previous factory legislation and laid down that all factories should be clean and hygienic and there should be proper fencing of machinery as well as improved ventilation and lighting. Shorter hours were gradually introduced with half-time working for children under fourteen. An Act of 1891 reinforced the regulations on fencing machinery and ventilation and the age at which a child could be employed in a factory was raised to eleven. The introduction of compulsory schooling in 1880 and free education in 1891 meant that far fewer children were working in the mills, although the age limit was not raised to twelve until 1901. The children's living conditions also gradually improved as local authorities in Watford and Hemel began to sort out the terrible problems of poor housing, inadequate water supplies and the absence of proper drainage. However, many of these housing problems, in both town and country, were not finally sorted out until the middle of the twentieth century.

Dickinson and Company continued in production in Hertfordshire into the twentieth century but by then conditions were very different from those prevailing in 1810 when Dickinson first set up his machinery at Apsley and Nash Mills. Croxley Mill closed in 1980 and Apsley Mill was turned into a paper warehouse and closed finally in 1999. Nash Mills was sold to another company and continues to make the well-known Croxley range of watermarked business paper so the tradition of papermaking in Hertfordshire continues to the present day.

Endnotes

1. A.H. Shorter, *Paper making in the British Isles* (Newton Abbot, 1971), p. 21.
2. J. Evans, *The endless web* (London, 1955), pp. 15–17.
3. BPP 1867–8 (4068) XVII.1.
4. BPP 1864 (3414) XXII.1; 1867–8 (4068) XVII.1.
5. Evans, *The endless web*, pp. 122–3.
6. BPP 1843 (431) XIV.1.
7. Evans, *The endless web*, p. 122.
8. *Watford Observer*, 3 May 1879.
9. BPP 1864 (3414) XXII.1; 1867–8 (4068) XVII.1.
10. Coutts Smith, *A Hertfordshire sampler*, pp. 144–5.
11. *Reports to the general board of health on the town of Watford, 1849–50.*

Chapter 6

Brickmaking

Background to brickmaking in Hertfordshire

The art of making bricks by baking moulded clay in kilns is very old, well-known in those parts of the ancient world without an abundance of stone. It was brought to the south-east of England by the Romans. Hertfordshire had no stone except flint, which was not easy to use for buildings. When the Romans left, the art of brickmaking was lost in England. In the first half of the fourteenth century there was a rapid increase in population with a need for many new dwellings; this ended for a while when the plague decimated the population in the second half of the century. It quickly revived in the fifteenth century and bricks were needed.

The process of making bricks

Brickfields were places where the clay was dug from the ground, moulded into bricks and baked in kilns. As bricks were so heavy to transport, the entire operation took place on a single site, chosen for its proximity to where buildings were to be erected. The county's clay deposits were close to chalk deposits that were also baked in kilns to provide lime as mortar for bricklaying or as fertiliser for arable land. Brickfields made tiles and chimney pots as well as bricks. Unlike Bedfordshire, Hertfordshire had few large-scale deposits of suitable clay apart from in the St Albans area, but it did have many small areas of clay and one or more could usually be found close to the place where buildings were needed. When large constructions were required, such as Hatfield House in the early seventeenth century and the Welwyn/Digswell railway viaduct in the mid-nineteenth century, small local brickfields opened up all round the sites.

Brickmaking[1] was largely a spring and summer activity, lasting from April to September in most years, when the clay was free of frost and heavy rain had stopped. In longer-lasting brickfields drying sheds were erected to protect the moulded bricks from rain until they were taken to the kilns. The moulded bricks were fired in kilns fuelled by wood or furze (gorse) at a very high temperature.

The digging of clay did, however, continue during the winter with the dug clay left on the surface, so that the frost could get into it and break it up, in the same way that farmers ploughed their fields in the autumn and left the harrowing until the spring when the frost had broken down the clumps into more workable soil. The adult male brickmaker doing the digging stood all day long in the cold water at the bottom of the pit, sometimes having to tunnel in the sides of the pit below the frost level. The sodden clay had to be lifted to the surface and this was very heavy work. It is no wonder that brickmakers were notoriously ill-tempered or that they sometimes took to heavy drinking.

Even after the frost had done its work, the clay had to be worked to make it more malleable and to remove stones before the brickmaker could use it. This process was called 'puddling' and was often done in a horse-powered 'pug mill', tended by a man called a 'tenderer'. If no pug mill was available the puddling was done by children tamping it with their feet (rather like treading grapes in a vineyard, except that it was much heavier work). Digging the clay was done by men. They thus continued to earn during the winter. In some areas the men had alternative work, such as malting in Ware and Bishop's Stortford. If neither digging nor an alternative were available, the men and their families had a very hard time at the period of the year when agricultural labourers were also without work. Then the workhouse became a possibility both for them and their families.

Brickmaking returns to Hertfordshire

When brickmaking resumed in Hertfordshire as elsewhere in Britain after its absence for centuries, the reputation of the county's brickmakers was quickly established and in the early sixteenth century some of them were summoned to make bricks for the construction of Hampton Court.

Brickmaking was an important industry employing children in many parts of the county but not everywhere. There had been many brickfields in Roman times and St Albans Abbey was built partly of brick reclaimed from ruined Roman buildings.[2] Two notable fifteenth-century brick buildings in Hertfordshire were the gate houses of Rye House, near Hoddesdon, and Hertford Castle. The grandest of Hertfordshire's grand houses, Hatfield House, built of brick by Robert Cecil in the early seventeenth century, required thousands of bricks to be made in the nearby brickfields. Many other houses were built of brick with some being 'improved' by the Victorians, who covered the brick with rendering (otherwise known as stucco).

Figure 25. Young boys and girls carrying clay from the pug mill to the brickmakers.

The huge rise in Hertfordshire's population in the nineteenth century was the spur to brickmaking. In 1801 there were 17,681 inhabited houses. By 1841 there were 89,155 and by 1881 406,932. Some of these dwellings were put up by jerry-builders. They were cramped together into the yards and courts of existing houses. The immediate need was to quickly provide housing for the labouring families in the papermaking and silk-throwing industries, as has been seen in earlier chapters. Similarly landowners had rushed to put up houses for their farm labourers. Many of these newly erected hovels had to be demolished in the slum-clearance reforms of the late nineteenth century and early twentieth century. Large numbers of bricks were also needed to erect the grand houses that the burgeoning bourgeoisie wanted in Hertfordshire to complement their London houses.

The work of children in Hertfordshire's brickfields

Hertfordshire children worked in brickfields in much of the county, doing most of the heaviest work, to 'service' their parents who moulded the bricks at tables. Many children, both boys and girls, were employed usually on a twelve-hour shift from seven in the morning until seven in the evening in mid-summer, moving the clay and the moulded and baked bricks through the various processes. As 'up-strikers', they carried the clay to the moulder. (The picture on the front of this book shows a girl doing such work). 'Off-strikers' loaded barrows. Barrowers were called 'off-bearers'. 'Pusher outers' carried the bricks from the kiln. If there was no horse-powered pug mill for making the clay malleable, children also had to tamp the clay to achieve the same end. Apart from digging the clay and operating the pug mill, if there was one, children provided most of the hard, unskilled labour.

In some parts of the county families had little choice but to work in this way in order to survive, although there is evidence that some of the fathers were well-paid but succumbed to the attractions of beer and gin.

Work versus schooling

The schools had little choice but to accommodate the wishes of the parents and the other employers that children should work in the brickfields rather than attend school. For example, on 23 May 1866 William Tiler was deemed by the teacher at St Mary's School, Ware to be worthy of a labour certificate to work in the brickfield.[3]

Labour certificates confirmed that a pupil had reached the required standard in attendance, reading, writing and arithmetic and needed no further schooling. Tiler had in fact left the school a year earlier and could not possibly have achieved the required attendance. The school was bowing to the inevitable and legitimising after the event what it had no means of resisting. Masters and mistresses had a strong incentive to take absentee pupils off the roll as this improved the school's recorded attendance rate, which affected their grants. Four days later another labour certificate was issued to W. Game whose attendance had been 'only fair'. The teacher commented that 'in winter and autumn the boys attend better. I have noticed these circumstances for many years.' Brickmaking was done only in the frost-free months, and when there was no heavy rain, usually from April until September.

Parental attitudes are exemplified by two cases on 21 November 1867 and 12 April 1869 when the teacher recorded:

> Chapman still refuses to attend the school and I have taken his name off the books. His father states that he will work in the brickfield rather than return to school.
>
> Presland, a very small boy has gone to work in the brickfield. His brother says that he will be here again if not equal to the work of barrow-loading.

There was another big problem related to the brickfield, that of unpunctuality, to which the school responded by changing the times of the morning session and even by sacrificing morning prayers. The teacher explained on 4 May 1867 that:

> Registers finally closed at 9.45. Instruction in secular subjects then directly commencing, this arrangement made temporarily in order that boys required to take dinners to the brickfield might be there by 12 the hour for dinner there then immediately beginning. For many years the taking of dinners to the brickfields has been a sore drawback to the summer morning attendance, several boys having made it their habit to lose their attendance altogether. Under these circumstances and with the consent of the vicar the above arrangement has been made. Work in the brickfield ceases about September.

Thus, even before they began to work in the brickfields themselves, boys had to leave school early at the end of the morning session or not attend in the first place in order to take their fathers' dinners to them. A similar arrangement was made the following year in April 1887, again with the approval of the vicar, which was needed as it was prayers that were forsaken and registration was followed immediately by secular lessons, thus allowing the morning session to finish early. Having taken their fathers' meals to the brickfields, many boys did not return to school for the afternoon session. Earlier that year on 28 April the teacher had bemoaned the poor attendance, noting that 'the brickfield is in operation again and has already much affected us. Several boys ... are there at work'.

There can be no doubt that the school in Ware was fighting against the economic realities of child labour in the brickfields. It was not alone. Parents needed their children to work or they would not have sufficient income to survive (although the more feckless brick moulders had enough money to spend on beer). This was a national problem for schools. It was not only boys who worked in the brickfields. In 1829 the mistress of Hitchin Girls' British School regretted that parents were taking their girls from school at such an early age and recorded several quitting during the year, among them 'Ann Hunt who was [wanted by her parents] to assist in the brickfields'.[4]

Despite attempts at reform, the brickfields were not covered by legislation until late in the century and even as late as the 1860s conditions for children working in brickfields had not improved. Extracts from the factory inspectors' annual report in 1866[5] reveal views that were at variance with each other. The gist of the favourable comments is that the children worked in the open air only in dry weather and looked swarthy and fit. Given the contrast with children working in cotton factories in the north of England, this view is understandable, but many children were malformed as a result of carrying heavy loads before their bodies, especially their bones and muscles, had matured.

The following extracts are from the report, compiled by one inspector using the reports of his colleagues. Where he quotes his fellow inspectors' comments directly or those of interviewees, these are shown in quotation marks. The varied comments include these:

> Children of both sexes are employed at a very early age in the brickfield. 'A moulder's child is born as the saying goes with a brick in his mouth. Many have begun work at 8 and 7 years.' 'Such are not, [as] is sometimes said, cases of children bringing their parents food and staying for perhaps an hour's time to relieve an older brother or sister.' 'I have myself met with many children, not 8 years age, working in the summer months as regular members of the moulder's gang day after day from 5am to 8pm.'
>
> 'In spite of their hard work children in brickfields, generally speaking, look strong and healthy. Though very ill-clothed they are well fed, and they work in the open air and not in wet weather. I suppose that is what keeps them, so healthy. I often wonder that they are not more generally injured but they certainly are not'. No! [interpolated the inspector compiling the report, in disbelief]. Similar words are used by another witness, who, though not in the business, had been for eight years constantly about the brickfields. 'I often wonder that the children can stand the work as they do, but nothing seems to hurt them they are as hardy as ground toads, as the saying is. Yet I have seen them so tired at the end of the day's work that the men have had to take them up in their arms to carry them home.
>
> The fact however is, that with all this appearance of rude health in the mass, there are not a few cases of positive physical injury produced by the exertion required in work wholly unfitted for children at so tender an age. This is particularly the case with the pusher-out, who has to carry from 210–270 lbs' weight of brick at a time on a one-wheeled spring barrow, to distance[s] sometimes of 50 yards and more. Both boys and girls have become crippled by beginning this too young. One lad had 'got his leg quite put out by it. So pug-boys have been ruptured by lifting too much for

Figure 26. A young girl barrower with a pug mill behind her.

their strength. A boy of about 12 years old 'pugging up' alone, will lift up from the ground from 30 to 40 lbs' weight of clay, and bear it a distance of five yards or more up an incline 120 times, sometimes 160 times, all in the course of an hour. Supposing the moulder to make 7,000 bricks to the day, each weighing 8 lbs, a fair average, the boy will have carried 25 tons a distance of five miles uphill, and have run another five miles downhill empty handed. *[Author's comment: The inspector seems to have taken estimates or the most extreme figures, indicated by the use of phrases such as ' a fair average', 'sometimes' and 'up to' for each aspect, and then put them into one calculation, making the speed of the task implausible. Some inspectors were thought to be biased, overstepping their role and themselves becoming reformers. This may be an example of over-zealous comment. It is understandable in the light of what the inspector had witnessed and what he wished to achieve, but not credible. The inspector should be given credit, nonetheless for reporting fairly the views of his colleagues that he himself found incredible.]* 'The same weight will have been lifted by the barrow-loader brick by brick; he is constantly lifting from the 'page to the barrow, a distance of from half a yard to a yard standing and swinging from one foot to another, and taking up the brick in both hands.'

> 'A girl, who began to load for her father at 9 years old, had at 13 a crooked ancle [*sic*] and a knee grown out on one side.' This man had three sons, the youngest only 8, at work with him, yet his wife told me that he actually kept this poor deformed child working in the field like the rest while he must have been clearing, with the help of his children, more than £4 a week after paying his temperer and off-bearer.

The importance of St Albans in Hertfordshire brickmaking

Dickens has provided us in *Bleak House* with an account of life in the St Albans brickfields, based on his own observation. The case of Charles Butcher is entirely factual.[6] Together they provide a picture of a harsh, bleak way of life in which drunkenness was a common feature.

Charles Butcher (14) was charged on remand with stealing £18, the property of his father, Charles Butcher the elder, and was tried at St Albans on the 14 August 1872. Amy Butcher said:

> I am the wife of Charles Butcher and reside in Catherines-lane ... I went to my son who was working at Mr Miskin's brickfield near Bernards Heath ... I said to George Bourn for whom the prisoner [referring to her son] works ... I [also] work for George Bourn and he pays me 7 shillings a week.

Others who worked for George Bourn in the brickfield were Samuel Bourn, Edward Dell and Henry Dell. It would appear that Charles Butcher gave the money to George and the others, who spent it on drink. Mr Blagg said he believes that they worked by the piece and not by the day. Mr Blagg said that 'being above 14 the bench could not order the prisoner to be whipped but he was liable to gaol with hard labour', which he was then given.

Three policemen, a prosecutor and three magistrates, including the mayor, were involved in the case. Apart from the harshness of the parents, who took the case against their own son with the mother giving the evidence, the case shows that adults were paid by the week while children were on piece work, that is paid by their output, and that in brickfields drinking beer was widespread among the young as well as their parents, stealing money having been the way in which the boys could fund their escapade. It is notable also that one of those taking part in the drinking spree was the son of the employer.

A literary portrayal of the living conditions of people working in the St Albans brickfields was given in *Bleak House* by Charles Dickens, a frequent visitor to the city and to other parts of the county such as Knebworth. Dickens was, of course, not only outraged by social injustice and the ill-treatment of the young but was also an accurate and astute observer at first-hand of inhumanity wherever he saw it, in this case family life in the St Albans brickfields. The brickfields, based on Dickens's knowledge of those at St Albans, play a crucial role in the plot of the novel. The heroine of the story, Esther Summerson, visited one with her friend Ada as members of a party organised by Mrs Pardiggle near the start of the novel and Lady Dedlock went to one, when exposed as the mother of the illegitimate Esther near the end of the novel when she wished to 'disappear', by exchanging clothes with a woman from the brickfield.

Most brickfields relied on brickmakers being supported by their families' labour. Dickens's portrayal of the unnamed brutal, drunken brickmaker, terrorising his cowed and sullen family, is confirmed by contemporary accounts to be accurate. Dickens was writing in 1853–5. The person telling the story in this extract is Esther Summerson:

> I was glad when we came to the brickmaker's house; though it was one of a cluster of wretched hovels in a brickfield, with pigsties close to the broken windows, and miserable little gardens before the doors, growing nothing but stagnant pools. Here and there, an old tub was put to catch the droppings of rain-water from a roof, or they were banked up with mud into a little pond like a large dirt-pie. At the doors and windows, some men and women lounged or prowled about, and took little notice of us, except to laugh to one another, or to say something as we passed about gentlefolks minding their own business, and not troubling their heads and muddying their shoes with coming to look after other people's.
>
> Mrs Pardiggle, leading the way with a great show of moral determination, and talking with such volubility about the untidy habits of the people (though I doubted if the best of us could have been tidy in such a place) conducted us into a cottage at the farthest corner, the ground-floor room of which we nearly filled. Besides ourselves, there were in this damp offensive room – a woman with a black eye, nursing a poor little gasping baby by the fire; a man, all stained with clay and mud, and looking very dissipated, lying at full length on the ground, smoking a pipe; a powerful young man, fastening a collar on a dog; and a bold girl, doing some kind of washing in very dirty water. They all looked up at us as we came in, and the woman seemed to turn her face towards the fire, as if to hide her bruised eye; nobody gave us any welcome.

'Now you're going to poll-pry and question according to custom. I know what you're a'going to be up to' (growled the man upon the floor). 'Well! You haven't got no occasion to be up to it. I'll save you the trouble. Is my daughter a-washin? Yes, she is a-washin. Look at the water. Smell it. That's wot we drinks. How do you like it, and what do you think of gin, instead? An't my place dirty? Yes, it is dirty – it's nat'rally dirty, and it's nat'rally onwholesome; and we've had five dirty and nat'rally onwholesome children, as is all dead infants, and so much the better for them and for us besides. Have I read that little book wot you left? No, I an't read the little book what you left. There an't nobody here as knows how to read it; and if there wos, it wouldn't be suitable to me. It's a book fit for a babby, and I'm not a babby. If you was to leave me a doll, I shouldn't muss it. How have I been conducting of myself? Why I've been drunk for three days; and I'd a been drunk four, if I'd a had the money. Don't I ever mean for to go to church? No, I don't ever mean for to go to church. I shouldn't be expected there, if I did; the beadle's too gen-teel for me. And how did my wife get that black eye? Why I give it her: and if she says I didn't, she's a Lie.'

The prevalence of alcohol in the lives of brickmakers, illustrated by both Dickens's characterisation and the Butcher case, was in part justified because drinking beer was thought to be healthier than drinking foul water. Widespread drunkenness and the general degradation of their lives were confirmed by factory inspectors. In 1872[7], one of them wrote:

I have found no class of men as ignorant as brickmakers, nor have the children, as a rule, ever gone to school or entered a place of worship.

In many places the foreman or master is a publican, so that whatever quantity of drink is required during the week it can easily be supplied. Wages are paid in the public-house; the landlady calls out each man's score, the week's earnings simply change hands from landlord and brickmaker to the landlady and the poor little children must wait for their very small portion till a balance is struck.

It is well known that they learn the habit of drinking at an early age, and are the sufferers from the inordinate lust for drink on the one side, and the rapacity of the publican on the other. I am told that as much as 15s a week is paid for drink by one man, whilst 5s represents the sum given to a wife for the support of a household.

> I went into a brickmaker's house in Norfolk, the man earned good wages, though he worked but four days a week. His wife was obliged to get a living for her family by laundry work, which barely sufficed, the children worked in the field with their father, from 4am to dark, for three or four days a week, but during the other days he was drinking. Out of 27s earned by him and his children the wife got 6d and a fourpenny loaf.

The earliest (Christian) reformers were outraged, not so much by the hard labour involved as by the immorality of the children, especially the girls, who, working among men, adopted their coarse and blasphemous language and gambling while flaunting themselves in front of the men. Reporting on the brickfields of Middlesex, the Rev. Dennett of Cranford wrote at length on the circumstances of the young people and commented.[8]

> ... the accommodation [is] provided by the brick moulder for his gang; this being a familiar practice in the industry. Such a situation was seen and described as [a] fruitful source of demoralisation [in modern parlance the term would be 'immoral behaviour']:
>
> Each moulder is supposed to lodge, board and 'do' for his gang of seven, and, if these are not all his own family, men, boys and girls sleep in his hut; this consists usually of two, sometimes three rooms, and all on the ground with very little ventilation. The bodies of all are greatly exhausted with the profuse perspiration of the day, so that neither health, cleanliness, nor decency can be much, if at all, regarded; and some of the huts are the perfection of untidiness, dirt and dust.

The great variety of brickfields in the county

Apart from the large brickfields at St Albans as observed above, brickfields in the county were broadly of five types.[9]

Some were on isolated sites needed for the construction of large houses such as Aldenham, Bayfordbury, Bricket Wood, High Cross, Great Munden and Queen Hoo or for big projects like the Digswell railway viaduct near Welwyn. Towns such as Braughing, Chorleywood, Hoddesden and London Colney had their own brickfields to provide for expansion. Others were also situated near towns, but with the additional attraction of new railway stations erected just outside the towns, with new housing developments between the stations and the towns, such as Boxmoor, Hemel Hempstead, Walsworth, Hitchin and Hertford. Very small fields were sometimes opened for specific purposes, often by farmers on their own land to build a few cottages and agricultural buildings. Short-lived brickfields were needed to construct railway tunnels and bridges, often using the clay that had been dug out to make the tunnels.

While the general characteristics of child labour in brickfields (hard and heavy work and long hours for low pay) were the same as in St Albans, in some fields there was not the same degradation and in most of the smaller fields a more wholesome family life was possible because most of the brickfields had only one or two brickmaking families. In others the mother or the family had employment other than as brickmakers.

Examples of short-lived brickfields abounded in the county. In the early nineteenth century John Nash of Potten End[10] became the tenant of Joseph Nash (possibly his father), using his four-acre plot for his house, garden, woodland and brickfield. There had been earlier brickfields in or near the village but by Nash's time these had reverted to farming. This shows how brickmaking could be easily started and stopped according to demand. Nash had a problem in finding fuel for his kiln. Although furze, the usual fuel, grew nearby, it was on the land of the Ashridge estate and the steward, Mr Atty, was already supplying brickfields at Coldharbour, Aldbury, Ashridge, Ivinghoe, and Kensworth and he needed to conserve the furze. Nash may just have ignored Atty's ban on the use of his furze, or he may have used wood from his own woodland or dried bracken. Whatever his solution, he started a successful business which ran for almost a hundred years. In 1851 Nash employed three men and by 1861 had added another man and three boys. His son, John Nash junior, took over the business and by the next decade had increased the workforce by four more men. An elderly man recalled ninety years later how his grandfather had been a digger of the clay in Nash's field and how he himself would take a pudding for his grandfather's meal and sit there while he ate it; this was similar to the habit of the Ware children already described. In the 1891 census John Nash junior was recorded as a 'retired brickmaker' and shortly afterwards sold his plot to a nurseryman.

Nash was not unusual. Thomas Little, who had the 433-acre Grange Farm near Tring, is shown in the 1881 census as employing sixteen males to work on the farm and nineteen making bricks. Thomas Franklin was a brickmaker first and only secondly a farmer at Bennett's End, Hemel Hempstead.[11] He described himself only as a brickmaker on the baptism certificate of his daughter in 1816 and on her marriage certificate in 1837.[12] Another such brickmaker was Frederick Albert Wood from 1896 to 1906 at the west end of Back Lane in Datchworth, a very small village. Many years later Mrs Skeggs recalled the brickfield established specifically to build some cottages. The brickmakers had to stay up all night to ensure that the kiln did not overheat.[13] Similarly, at Ashwell John Chapman was both a farmer and a brickmaker in 1850 and 1851 but before that in 1839 and afterwards in 1854 he was shown in trade directories as just a farmer. His brickfield was an example of the very small and short-lived brickfields brought into being to meet a modest local demand. The close link between farming and brickmaking was noted in the report of an inspector to the Agriculture Commission in 1867. He reported that there was no complaint about the labour of children in the farm fields but added, almost as an aside, that both the vicar and the schoolmaster suggested that 'interference [that is, regulation] was needed in the brickfield, where children of 6 and 7 work barefooted' all day.[14]

The Digswell/Welwyn viaduct is an example of a large brickfield created for a specific purpose. The Digswell or Welwyn Viaduct was constructed across the Mimram Valley to carry the railway from King's Cross station in London to the new station of Welwyn North, but was always intended to become a line to York in the minds of the directors of the Great Northern Railway Company. The building of the viaduct was a great engineering feat, opposed by George Hudson, a railway millionaire, not only because he thought that it would be impossible to build, saying that 'if they try to build a bridge across the Mimram Valley, every penny of their capital will disappear in a waterlogged swamp' but also because he was making his fortune from his railways in the midlands and the north and did not want his monopoly to be undermined. The viaduct was built by the great engineer, Thomas Brassey, whose services were in demand throughout the world, including France where Brassey had earlier taken his gang of navvies to build the Paris to Rouen railway in 1841. The arrival of Brassey, who took up residence in the Cowpers Arms, Welwyn, while his navvies moved into a huge encampment of shacks stretching from Digswell to Digswell Farm at Black Fan Lane, caused quite a stir in the area, not least because the navvies had picked up some French words, albeit imperfectly, becoming known as the 'tray bong' gang. One of the entertainments they provided for themselves and the locals was the bare-knuckle prize fighting that they staged behind the Duck at Burnham Green on Friday nights.

The number of bricks required for the viaduct has been estimated very differently. Tony Rook[15] has done the most careful research on the matter and estimated it at almost fourteen million between 1847 and 1850. The bricks were made on site.

The Waller family were the largest brickmakers in Digswell/Welwyn throughout the century. James Waller, as the tenant of Lord Cowper, made bricks in Digswell in

Figure 27. Digswell/Welwyn viaduct, 1864. Almost fourteen million bricks made on site were needed to build the viaduct between 1848 and 1850.

1840. George Waller, calling himself a brickmaker and a bricklayer, lived in Digswell from 1832 to 1839. It is known that he bought furze, the fuel used for firing brick in kilns, from a Codicote farmer named Sapte, because in 1834 a rick of furze that he had bought caught fire.[16] Sapte planted and harvested the crop much as other farmers did with hay. George Waller leased land from the Wilshere family. There was also a James Waller who was a brickmaker at Digswell Water from 1864 until 1866, long after the viaduct had been completed and was in use.[17]

Several towns experienced considerable population growth and building construction in the nineteenth century. Hitchin is a well-documented example of those towns affected by the arrival of a railway and the building of a station just outside the town at Walsworth. By 1861 one in thirteen Hitchin adult males were working in the building trades. By 1901 this had risen to one in eight; it was a veritable boom in the building industry requiring many bricks.[18]

The brickmaking business was quite different in Hitchin from that in St Albans. The owners and controllers of brickmaking were mostly very respectable men in the town, often members of the Society of Friends (Quakers) with social consciences and civic pride. They did not tolerate the degradation described by Dickens. They were also shrewd businessmen. They engaged family brickmakers to do the work.

There was no large continuous area of suitable clay in Hitchin except for a sixty-four feet length of clay in Bethel Street (now St John's Road). There were, however, several important separate areas with much clay and with ample chalk as well. Hitchin's brickfields and yards served relatively small areas close to their operations. In the area between the Folly (now the Stevenage Road) and Blackhorse Lane the Jeeves family were for many years important brickmakers with a yard in Dead (now Queen) Street and a chalk pit in the Whitehill area. Another significant area was Hitchin Hill, where James Rave and the Pitt family were brickmakers. At Bearton G. Pierson, was the tenant of William Wilshere. John Ransom was the largest of the town's brickmakers and lime-burners with a brickyard in Nightingale Road and brickflelds in Long Ing Close (later Seven Acres) at Bearton.[19] John and Thomas Pitt had brickfields on Hitchin Hill from 1882 to 1886, making red bricks. For much of the nineteenth century James Rave had a yard in Bridge Street, and a brickfield and chalk pit near the Stevenage Road.

The terms 'brickmaker', 'brickyard owner' (now called a builders' merchant), 'bricklayer' and 'builder' were not so clearly defined and separate as they are now; they were almost interchangeable, as many firms embraced all of them. An unusual combination of roles was that of Thomas Pearson (1844), a solicitor and also a tile and brickmaker of Park Street, Hitchin Hill and Queen Street.[20] It is not difficult to see the link between being a solicitor and a brickmaker/builder as being that of property transfer.

Many of the sons of the family brickmakers engaged by these businesses attended school and did not become just adjuncts to their fathers, who were paid enough to be able to forego income from their sons' labour and in many cases were married to better-paid straw-plaiters, so that they could afford to pay the school fees. Amongst the eight sons of brickmakers enrolled at Hitchin British School[21] were: Jasper Marley of the Folly in 1833; George Lewis, aged nine, of Church Yard, whose father was working for Mr A Ransom in 1871; Jasper Manning, aged thirteen and his brother Alfred, aged eleven of Benslow Hill, which was an important area for lime-burning; and George Potter of the Folly in 1870 whose father had moved around, also living and making bricks at Hitchin Hill, Highbury and Bearton.

If the 1851 census summary of occupations is to be taken at its face value, there were no longer any females, child or adult, working in the brickfields. This was a drop from three girls under twenty years of age shown in the equivalent table in the 1841 census. In 1851 there were thirty-four males under the age of fifteen working in brickmaking in Hitchin.

There were many references to the evils of child labour in the brickfields by factory inspectors and by witnesses to parliamentary committees of enquiry during the century. Nonetheless, it was not until the last quarter of the century that the passage

Figure 28. George Smith, the great campaigner against child labour.

of Education Acts had a significant impact. These made school attendance compulsory, albeit still part-time, and free for children up to eleven years of age and later twelve. Then the problem was adequately tackled, making it difficult for parents to have their children at any work. Even then action to enforce the law was largely dependent on the local school boards. Referring back to near the start of this chapter, it is notable that the Ware board was among the most active in pursuing non-attendance between 1877 and 1892.[22]

It is worth remembering why it was so important to reform child labour in the brickfields. George Smith[23], who campaigned tirelessly on behalf of the brickfield children, had been a brickfield child himself in the late 1840s. He started work at the age of nine when he was made to carry about forty pounds of clay or bricks for thirteen hours daily, walking up to fourteen miles in the course of his week's work. He never forgot the misery of his early life and was determined to rescue children from such heavy labour. In 1869 as part of his campaign he had a brickfield child of about nine weighed. The child weighed fifty-two and a half pounds but was made to carry about forty pounds of clay on his head. Smith was not as well known as the Earl of Shaftesbury but for children made to work in the brickfields he was of equal importance. His success came with the Factories and Workshops Amendment Act of 1871 that banned the employment of boys under ten and girls under sixteen from working in the production of bricks and tiles. Accidents involving loss of life or bodily injury had to be notified to the authorities; this was a period when the importance of regulations and safety rules was appreciated.

Endnotes

1. L. Perrins, 'Recalling Hertfordshire's brickworks', *Hertfordshire Countryside*, 36 (April 1981), p. 27.
2. For a more detailed explanation of brickmaking see the unpublished work, Chris Reynolds, 'The history of Bernards Heath, St Albans', available at http://www.hertfordshire-genealogy.co.uk/data/projects/brick-makers-talk/brickmakers/making-bricks.htm.
3. Log book of St Mary's School, Ware, HALS, D/P 116.
4. Eleventh annual report of Hitchin girls' British schools, HALS, D/P 67531.
5. BPP 1866 (3678) XXIV.1, *Children's employment commission* (1862).
6. *St Albans Advertiser*, 24 August 1872, cited by C. Reynolds, 'History of Bernards Heath'.
7. BPP 1873 (c.745) XIX.41, *Reports of inspectors of factories to Secretary of State for Home Department, May–October 1872*, pp.19–20.
8. A. Bennett, *A working life: child labour through the nineteenth-century*, 2nd edn (Launceston, 1995), p. 51.
9. L. Perrins, 'Hertfordshire brickworks: a gazetteer', *Hertfordshire Archaeology and History*, 14 (2004–05), pp. 187–296.
10. Bryant, Potten End, p. 45.
11. *Hertfordshire county directory for 1850*, HALS.
12. Additional information provided by Judith White, four times granddaughter of Franklin, from the registers of the parish church in Hemel Hempstead, HALS.
13. Beachcroft and Emms, *Five hide village*, p. 185.
14. BPP 1867–8 (4068) XVII.1.
15. T. Rook, 'Welwyn viaduct', *The Welwyn Times*, 28 July 1959.
16. E. L. Lawrence, *Diary of a village* (*Codicote*), typed copy in Hitchin Library, ref H45 376 660 9 amended 1998, entry for 15 November 1834, pp. 43–5.
17. Perrins, 'Hertfordshire brickworks'.
18. T. Crosby, P. Douglas, S. Fletcher, M. Gimson, B. Howlett, P. Humphries and S. Walker, *Jeeves Yard: a dynasty of Hitchin builders and brickmakers* (Baldock, 2003), pp. 43–5; Perrins, 'Hertfordshire brickworks'.
19. Perrins, 'Hertfordshire brickworks'.
20. *Ibid.*
21. Hitchin boys' British school index of admissions.
22. Ware school attendance committee minute book, HALS, BG/WAR/102.
23. G. Smith, *Cry of the children from the brickyards of England* (Coalville, 1880).

Chapter 7

Chimney-sweeping

The child assistants of chimney-sweeps, mostly boys but sometimes girls, were described by the great factory reformer, the Earl of Shaftesbury, on 11 May 1875 as 'thousands of the most oppressed, degraded and tortured creatures on the face of the earth', when seeking support for the Second Reading of his Bill in the House of Lords for what was to become the first effective act to protect sweep children. That was after almost a hundred years of ineffective legislation intended to improve their lot.

Climbing chimneys was a peculiarly dreadful way of life, suited only to small children, either very young or undernourished. For most of the children there was no escape, as they worked for their own father sweeps or for sweeps who apprenticed them direct from the workhouse.

In Hertfordshire most families employed their own children, sometimes supplemented by other people's children and occasionally with the addition of journeymen (adult sweeps paid by the day) but the children of the master sweeps were the most valued because, when young and small, they could be sent up chimneys. Also the members of the family did not need to receive wages, so that all the income from sweeping chimneys went into the family income without dilution. The children themselves were not paid.

Census returns for Hertfordshire show that 32 per cent of sweeps were under the age of fifteen in 1841, 25 per cent in 1851 and 19 per cent in 1861, but by 1871 this had fallen to less than 5 per cent. Although there is some evidence of female sweeps, not climbing girls, at Hadley and Barnet at the beginning of the century, by the 1851 census the only female sweeps in Hertfordshire were widows or adults working with their husbands in the business.

There are grounds for suspecting that the 1851 returns understated the number of young children climbing chimneys in Hertfordshire by recording them as 'scholars'.

Figure 29. A sweep calling for trade, 1866.

There had been some well-publicised cases in the previous decade of sweeps being prosecuted or warned by magistrates for sending boys up chimneys and word would have spread throughout the county's colony of sweeps and stopped them from being too open with the census enumerators in 1851. There was an unusually high number of boy 'scholars' in sweep families, which seems an unlikely 'occupation' for sweeps' sons. Census enumerators recorded whatever information they were given and had no right to check its veracity or any means of doing so. Sweep boys would not in any case have been accepted in any schools except the Ragged Schools and most sweeps were too poor to pay the fees of the National (Church of England) or the British (dissenting) schools, which did not welcome children who were dirty, poorly clad and poorly shod.

There were sweep families in all the main urban centres where there were older large houses in the town or nearby. Apart from Hertford and Hitchin, which had the largest numbers of sweeps, Barnet, Berkhamsted, Hemel Hempstead, St Albans, Royston, Tring and Watford all had at least one sweep family and some also combined it with smaller businesses like collecting night soil, selling soot for fertiliser and bricklaying.

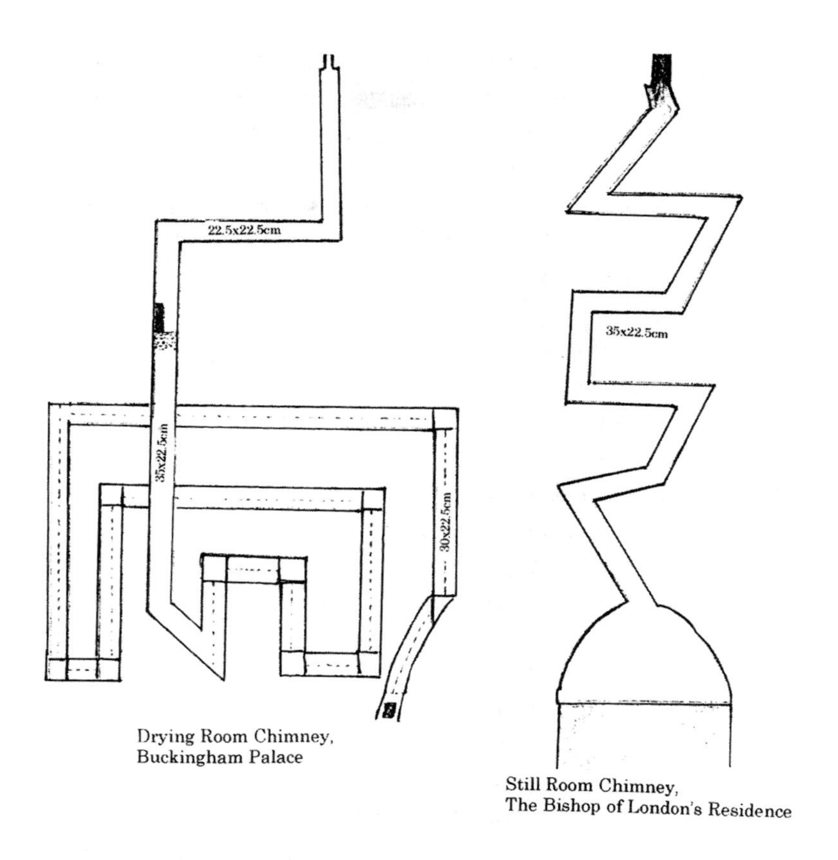

Figure 30. The complicated flues the climbing boys had to negotiate.

Several Hertfordshire sweep families, for example the Dyes of Hertford, the Howards of Hitchin, the Rayments of Royston and the Garments of Aldbury (near Tring) were in business throughout the century, becoming the dominant sweeps in their areas.

The living and working conditions of child climbing boys severely affected their health and life expectancy. They had virtually no education, except perhaps an occasional attendance at a Ragged or Sunday school. Misshapen and deformed by edging their way up narrow flues using their knees and elbows and having to squeeze past very tight bends, few child sweeps were employable beyond their late teens or early twenties, unless they became master sweeps themselves.

The lives of climbing boys were wretched. Many contracted lung and testicular cancers, the latter commonly known to doctors as sweeps' wart or sweeps' cancer, whatever its origin. All had respiratory diseases. Many had open, untreated wounds and bone and muscular problems. The routine preparation to harden the boys' knees and elbows was rigorous rubbing with brine, itself a painful process. The Earl of Shaftesbury in his speech to the Lords noted above referred to another practice as a treatment to prevent infection in open wounds. This was to apply 'netting', a concoction made from old urine in which cinders had been simmered. It was even more painful than using brine to harden the skin over joints; children would howl in pain. Mostly the boys went naked up the chimneys to prevent their clothes from catching on the stacks or on the soot and bringing it down in an uncontrolled manner; the aim was to climb to the top of the flue before working their back way down to the hearth.

Yet, there were examples in Hertfordshire of climbing boys surviving all these horrors and living to a great age, mainly if they had younger siblings to take over their wretched job before they themselves had succumbed to its hazards.

Housing conditions

Sweeps in the two towns where the majority of them lived, Butcherly Green in Hertford and Hollow Lane in Hitchin, occupied the worst houses. William Ranger, the Superintendent Inspector of the General Board of Health, reported[1] on the two areas in 1849–50 as follows:

Of Hertford he wrote:

> Cesspool under human dwellings and the effluvium so offensive that parties could not occupy their lower rooms; dung-heaps, pigsties and unpaved yard, with foul water lying stagnant upon the surface; fluid excrement soaking into outhouses; privies exposed and open to all comers; occupiers of blocks of houses, deprived of water [other than rain water collected from roofs] for several years. In other cases, the soil from privies soaks into the wells; pigs and manure-heaps adjoining walls and near to windows and doors of human dwellings; foul water and sewerage, overflowing. Barrels on wheels the only privies in some courts; groups of privies, in a filthy state over one common cesspool, in the midst of dwellings; in many places there was a great want of privies [which were] in a dreadful and filthy state ... heaps of dung and accumulations of offal from slaughter-houses; deposits of foul stagnant water.

It was also stated that in various places the people complained of being constantly ill. One person, having resided in the locality for eighteen years, said that some of the family had suffered from sickness during the whole period. Not surprisingly, the

Figure 31. Butcherly Green in Hertford where the Dye family and other sweeps lived.

inspector had some difficulty in knowing where to begin in making recommendations. It is hardly surprising that in 1832 twenty-seven people in Hertford died from cholera as a result of polluted water, with seventy deaths from it in 1849.[2]

Of Hollow Lane, Hitchin, Ranger wrote:

> 24 houses, only 8 having outlets at back, and a family consisting of 13 persons [who] reside in a house comprising but two sleeping rooms; and in other houses, the number varies from 7 to 9 persons, with but one sleeping room in each house...
>
> There are four privies to 24 houses, occupied by 136 persons. These privies are used in common by the occupiers of 20 houses; the inhabitants of the remaining four houses have no privies.

Figure 32. Goldings, the house where, in 1844, James Dye was suffocated to death, 1860.

This is what the climbing boys of the two towns left behind early each morning to go to work and what they returned to each day after work. Their working and living conditions were in different ways equally bad. It was rare for sweep children not living with their own families to have a bed on which to sleep; more often they slept in the basement of the sweeps' houses on soot bags or in the attic on straw. The 1841 census showed two sweep boys, Michael Kingseller aged fifteen and an unnamed boy aged eleven sleeping in stables at Butcherly Green. Shameful though that was, they might have considered themselves fortunate to have some shelter although they lived like animals.

The death of James Dye, climbing boy of Hertford, at Goldings in 1844

In the 1875 debate in the House of Lords, Shaftesbury referred to several cases of climbing boys having been suffocated up chimneys. He did not mention the death of James Dye junior that had occurred in Hertfordshire in 1844. In the nineteenth century the Dyes were the most prominent family of Hertford sweeps, established in the 1830s at Green Street, in the Butcherly Green part of the town, where all the sweep families lived. In the long run it was by far the most successful as a business, notwithstanding an early disaster. James Dye senior was the head of the family when one of his climbing boys, his own son, also named James and aged ten at the time, died from suffocation having been trapped in a flue at Goldings, a country mansion at Waterford just outside Hertford.

In 1844 the house was owned by Lord Reay and was also the home of his son-in-law, Sir Minto Farquhar, who had tried unsuccessfully to become MP for Hertford in 1830 and was later to succeed in becoming one of the borough's two MPs. According to his obituary, Farquhar took an interest in the welfare of working men and a particular interest in that of boys. He 'took a great interest in all schemes for promoting education and ... he was ever ready to help boys who showed diligence to promote themselves in life.'[3]

The passage of the Chimney Sweeps – Climbing Boys Act in 1840 is relevant to the case, although the law was not implemented until July 1842. Popular hostility to the use of climbing boys was so strong that the House of Commons approved the bill without debate and the consciences of some peers including the bishops led them to support it in the Lords. As always happened with legislation on climbing boys before Shaftesbury's Act of 1875, the main opposition came from peers, representing the interests of the owners of large London and country houses with complicated flues. The delaying tactic of referring the matter to a Select Committee of Lords in response to a petition from London master sweeps was approved with a majority of seventeen, a surprisingly close vote, showing how strong the case for reform was. The tactic backfired, however, and the evidence collected encouraged support for the bill. The delay in implementation by more than a year was a partial success for its opponents. More important was the fact that the main clause, banning the use of climbers under the age of twenty, if implemented in effect meant a ban on climbing boys altogether since few people aged twenty, however ill-nourished, could climb up flues. The Act was effective for the first few years after 1842 before being largely ignored like its predecessors.

It proved difficult at the time to be certain of the facts in the case of James Dye's death and has remained so since. The involvement of such important people (the local peer and the would-be local MP) may have contributed to this.

The Dyes were surely in a difficult position, since it was they who had sent their own son up the chimney against the law. The Hertford coroner, Thomas Sworder, conducted the inquest at Goldings itself in the presence of the boy's body. Emotion and self-justification may well have helped to obscure the simple facts. Like most of the inhabitants of Butcherly Green, the Dyes were tenants of the gentry because most of the houses there were owned by the Marquess of Salisbury, Baron Dimsdale or other owners of large mansions. These and the Abel Smith family, who lived nearby, were the Dyes' potential customers and word would have gone swiftly round if the Dyes became troublesome.

There were two main accounts of what happened, but with a degree of concurrence: that of the coroner's inquest as reported in the local paper, the *Hertfordshire Mercury*, on 5 July 1844, which was of course contemporary and immediate, and a second account, a century later, presumed to have been based on the family's version, as published in *The Nines*, the magazine of the Hertfordshire Fire and Ambulance Service. Unfortunately, the official report of the coroner's hearing has not survived. The family version was repeated as an article by the boy James's great nephew and was later reprinted in an official history of Hertford in 1959.[4] It has since been widely repeated but needs to be regarded with caution as it was an oral account passed through the family generations before finally being committed to paper.

James's death certificate recorded his demise as taking place at 4am on 5 July 1844. What is agreed is that one of the boy's parents (whether his mother, herself a sweep, or his father differs in the accounts) took James to Goldings early in the morning on the day of the tragedy, once the flues had cooled overnight, and sent him up from the kitchen hearth. After a while James called down that he was stuck. His parent told him to climb to the top of the flue. When he could not move up or down, a mason was called who broke through several walls until he found James's dead body. It was thought that James had tried to climb a flue leading nowhere, perhaps originally intended for a fireplace that was not built. When he was found he was immersed in soot and presumed by the physician to have suffocated.

The family version is dramatic, if not melodramatic. It has the boy's mother, not father, as the one in charge, arriving with their donkey (an essential member of all sweeps' teams for carrying the brushes and afterwards for carrying away the soot) and the boy at 3.30am. Having sent James up the flue, she went outside to await his call from the chimney above. Returning to the kitchen, she heard him calling that he was stuck. This version had the boy's age as seven, which would clearly have been illegal even under the 1788 law, let alone the more recent Act of 1840. She judged that it was too early to awaken the family to seek their help, a cruel dilemma for a mother at that time: whether to defer to her customer's comfort or save her son's life. She set off to Hertford to seek help, cutting through the grounds in the morning darkness, and prolonging her journey by falling into the river. This account does not finish the story.

The newspaper account of the coroner's enquiry says that the coroner was initially minded to have James Dye senior indicted for manslaughter, but had come to the conclusion that a penalty of £10, the maximum fine allowed under the 1840 Act for sending the boy up the flue, would be sufficient. The jury returned a verdict of 'accidental death' after some more (unreported) comments from the coroner.

Lord Reay made a statement to the coroner that he had specifically told James's father not to use a climbing boy. That seems a very odd thing for him to have said as Lord Reay knew that the use of climbing boys was a routine part of chimney-sweeping and the House of Lords was where most abolition measures foundered because peers like Reay were the owners of the mansions most in need of climbing boys. Reay would have known that under the 1840 Act the client had as much responsibility as the sweep to enforce the ban on climbing. If this were a dishonest, post-tragedy invention by Reay to the coroner, Dye would not have challenged it. In an age of social deference, sweeps, who were regarded as 'sub-trade', did not denounce peers of the realm as liars. If Reay did make his statement, James senior may have ignored his injunction in order to obtain the work, given the need to feed his family. Sweeps generally were harsh masters, although it is not known whether this was the case with James Dye senior, and were among the most poorly paid workers, so not able to turn down a job.

The other important discrepancy is the age of the boy James, with the family version giving it as seven and the death certificate as ten. Whether James was seven or ten, nobody, least of all Reay and Farquhar, an existing and an aspirant parliamentarian, could have thought that he was twenty. If the boy was either of these ages, his father as his employer and Lord Reay as the customer were both breaking the law and it may have been this that concerned Lord Reay and the boy's father equally.

Another factor that could have influenced James senior was that he would certainly have wanted to win more big contracts in the county, not least one with the Marquess of Salisbury, whose contract he secured some years later to clean the flues of Hatfield House four times a year for the sum of £40 a year for this multi-chimneyed mansion. The Dyes still had the contract in 1910.

James Dye senior was still in charge of the business in 1851 when the census showed that he was assisted by his eleven-year-old son, William. James Dye senior lived to the age of sixty-two. His other son, Daniel, aged five, was said to be a 'scholar' in the 1851 census but his schooling was not to last much longer. It is known from an interview given to the *Hertfordshire Mercury* on 24 February 1939 when he was in his nineties that Daniel also became a sweep:

> Daniel said 'I was barely eight years old when my father [James Dye senior] took me out working for him for the first time. I didn't look forward to it as one of my brothers [James junior] had suffocated to death when climbing up the inside of a chimney but it was the general thing for a sweep's son to do. My father had done it for his father and there seemed no reason why I shouldn't too'.

Figure 33. Another member of the Dye family, maybe David Dye, after his initiation into the job by having his face dipped in a bag of soot. The photograph was probably taken in the late nineteenth century about fifteen years after children had stopped climbing chimneys to clean them, instead using brushes and rods like those the boy is holding.

If the Dye chimney-sweeping business consisted just of the father and one son in 1851, it is possible that it had been adversely affected by the Goldings incident, for Daniel was spared James's climbing life for a while. If the incident did cause some loss of trade, the family business recovered and it continued until the twentieth century as the pre-eminent sweep business in Hertford and its surroundings. The *Hertfordshire Mercury* of 17 May 1940 reported that Daniel was buried at All Saints Church, where he had been a sidesman for some years; this in itself shows something of a social breakthrough by the family.

The Dye family flourished in Hertford and its environs before leaving the trade behind it. The member of the family writing the account in the twentieth century of James Dye's death, when the firm had become much more respectable and climbing boys were a thing of the past, was mayor of Hertford in two consecutive years and an alderman of Hertford Borough; he also became a member of Hertfordshire County Council. A member of the family who graduated in the twentieth century and became deputy headteacher of a large comprehensive school in the county remembers going with his sweep father, just to watch the brush appear at the top of the chimney, not to

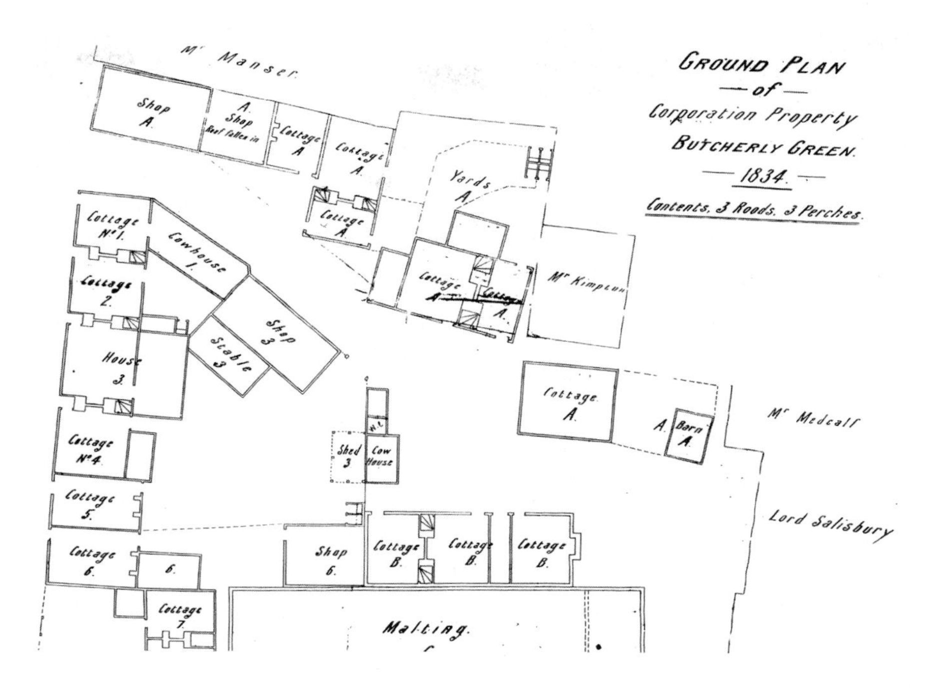

Figure 34. A plan of the slums of Butcherly Green, 1834.

work. Thus the family had risen from 'the poorest of the poor' to become a family that included a businessman holding civic office and another member of the family holding a senior position in one of the county's schools.

Other breaches of the law by Hertford sweeps

The 1851 census shows four other family chimney-sweeping businesses in Hertford, two of which had appeared before the courts for infringements of the law.

Joseph Baker and his wife employed their ten-year-old son, Joseph junior, and eight-year-old nephew, John Saunders from Essex, and two other sweeps, Samuel Jones from Stoke Newington, Middlesex, and Raiserra Sattina, a thirteen-year-old boy from Hertfordshire (town not recorded). They also had a labourer and his family lodging in the house, indicating the need for a supplementary income.

In the *Hertfordshire Mercury* of 2 April 1847 it was reported that Baker had been charged with assaulting Samuel Criple, his 'hired servant'. The boy himself was the complainant. He was described by the newspaper reporter as 'a diminutive boy apparently aged about eleven, with handsome features begrimed with soot and attired in ragged and sooty clothes'. Small he may have been but courageous he certainly was to accuse his master before a court. It emerged during the hearing that Criple was on a yearly hiring with no apprenticeship and that he claimed to be sixteen. By not giving Criple an apprenticeship Baker was at least in that regard abiding by the 1840 Act, which had abolished apprenticeships to sweeps. The mayor, who was also the presiding magistrate, was incredulous to hear the boy's claimed age. The boy's charge was that his master, 'angry at some trifling neglect on his part, had beaten him mercilessly and inflicted blows upon his head, which was severely cut'. Baker admitted the assault and confessed that he had not yet honoured an undertaking to the boy's mother to find him clothes. Criple came from London where his mother lived in Brick Lane but no explanation was sought or offered on how he had come to be in Hertford. The purchase of small children by sweeps was known as a particular evil of the trade but this possibility can be only speculation in Criple's case. The mayor was quite clear that Baker had done wrong, saying that he had no right to touch the boy. His verdict was, however, to give Baker a week in which to provide the boy with clothes, to re-present the boy to him the following Monday after he had had a wash (which was normally done only on Sundays if at all) and also to get the boy to attend church. If Baker were to do these things he would escape a fine. The requirement of church attendance followed an odd exchange between the mayor and Baker, who gave a 'rambling account of the way in which Criple preferred to play with other boys on Sundays instead of going to church'. The mayor then put Baker on the spot and asked whether he himself attended church on Sundays. Reluctantly Baker admitted that he did not. The mayor said 'The best way of seeing that he goes to a place of worship is to take him yourself. You will not regret it.' By that stage the serious assault and serious breach of the 1840 Act seemed to have been almost forgotten and exposure to the scriptures regarded as more effective than law enforcement. There is no evidence to show where Criple lived at the time of the assault; not surprisingly, Criple was not living with Baker in 1851 and he does not appear anywhere else in the Butcherly Green part of the census.

Edward Bland senior, born in Baldock and aged sixty-four in 1851 at the time of the incident in which he was involved, was assisted by his forty-year-old son, James, and by two boy sweeps from Highgate, then in Middlesex, called Isaac Angella, aged sixteen, and Henry Angella, aged nine. Another boy sweep called Henry Squires, aged nine, also worked for him. In 1851 Squires was brought before the court in Hertford when it became clear that Bland had offended against the 1840 Act. The *Hertfordshire Mercury* reported on 25 October 1851 that:

> A little boy Squires, not quite nine-years-old was brought up on charges of stealing glasses from a cart in the market ... The owner of the glasses refused to prosecute the boy. After being severely reprimanded by the mayor Squires was discharged. Before he left the room, Mr Gilbertson asked if he was in the habit of sweeping chimneys and on his replying in the affirmative, Mr Gilbertson told him to inform his master (Mr Bland) that if he continued to go up chimneys, he would have him fined. The Mayor said he thought the public were not generally aware that any person might be fined £5 for sending a boy up a chimney. The law affected not only the master of the boys but extended to the public. He thought that the law was very much violated in this neighbourhood. Squires (the father of the boy) said that machines were of no use in some chimneys. Mr Gilbertson said that the law made no exceptions, and the parties were bound to have the chimneys of their houses altered to make the machines effectual and not allow boys to go up them.

The magistrate, knowing that an offence had been committed, colluded with the father and the sweep in issuing just a warning against future infringements to be delivered to the master by proxy (the little boy himself). He had at least used the situation to issue a general warning to the public, including householders, letting them know that they, as well as the sweep, could be found guilty. The 1840 Act had by this time been in force for almost a decade and yet, to the mayor's knowledge, was still being ignored widely in the town.

Thus of the five master sweeps in the county town, three (James Dye, Joseph Baker and Edward Bland) had broken the law.

Some boy sweeps, but not in Hertfordshire as far as is known, were even bought from their parents or taken from the workhouse to sweep chimneys. Evidence was given by a Leicester magistrate to the Children's Employment Commission that there were 'great numbers of these children regularly bought and sold and that they were as completely slaves as any negro children of South Carolina'. The witness went on to say that he and his fellow Leicester magistrates had dealt with a case of two illegitimate children, aged six and eight years, being taken to a chimney sweeper under false pretence from a workhouse.[5]

Reformers and self-help

The lives of climbing boys were indeed grim but in Hertfordshire the boys were not without friends and supporters and there were sometimes ways out of extreme poverty for their families.

IMPROVED METHOD
OF
Sweeping Chimneys.

THE evils attending the usual mode of Sweeping Chimneys have long been known and deeply deplored. Children are taken at an early age and devoted to this cruel and dangerous employment; by these means some of the little sufferers have lost their lives in a manner shocking to humanity; others have been maimed for life; many have been subject to an incurable disease, which has embittered and shortened their days; and the whole system has a tendency to debase the morals of those who are thus employed; rendering them unsuitable to associate with society, besides unfitting them for getting a livelihood when grown too large to be further used in this degrading occupation.

A Meeting will be held in the Assembly Room, at the Sun Inn, Hitchin, on Wednesday Morning, the 29th instant, at half-past Eleven o'Clock; for the purpose of exhibiting and explaining a Machine invented for Cleansing Chimneys, which removes the soot as effectually as the usual method.

Figure 35. Notice of a meeting to be held at the Sun Inn, Hitchin, on 29 April 1829, to draw attention to a new machine for cleaning chimneys. The aim was to put pressure on master sweeps to use the machine instead of climbing boys but the campaigners had to wait another forty-five years to achieve their objective.

One route followed by reformers at the beginning of the nineteenth century was to argue for the use of machines rather than climbing boys but even a society that had the King as patron trying to find a machine that could eliminate the need for climbing boys made no headway, although it evoked support for its aims in Hitchin and Hertford, the Hertfordshire towns with the most sweeps.

In June 1829 a meeting was held in Hitchin at the assembly rooms of the Sun Hotel, at which it was agreed to set up a branch of the national society. This was the society, called the Society for Superseding the Necessity for Climbing Boys (SSNCB), that enjoyed royal patronage, perhaps rather hypocritically, since Buckingham House (as it was then called) used more climbing boys than most buildings, although probably no more than the Houses of Parliament. Both of these buildings could have been adapted to take machines, which was the solution later required by the 1840 Act and was being canvassed long before then. The Hitchin meeting, chaired by the vicar, the Reverend Henry Wiles, was very confident that machines could replace climbing boys and it set up a fund with donations from the ninety-two attendees, who gave pledges to buy the machines and undertakings to use them in their own houses.[6]

Hertford followed this route in 1832 when an article appeared in the *Hertfordshire County Press* on 24 February recording financial support for a machine being used by R. Waller, a bricklayer who lived in Fore Street, Hertford, and who claimed to have swept ten chimneys a week for ten months using it. Waller's efforts were supported by a Hertford group established to promote the sweeping of chimneys by machines. Their accounts showed that they had raised enough money to buy the machine and pay Waller's wages for sweeping chimneys using it, leaving £2 over for a donation to the London Society that shared their aims (presumed to be the SSNCB or it may have been the Society of Arts, Manufacture and Commerce, later to become the Royal Society of Arts (RSA), which had organised competitions to find effective machines). Both towns were ahead of their times in that they were promoting desirable change, unsupported by legislation.

Hitchin returned to the fray after the 1840 Act came into force, printing large posters quoting the main part of the Act and stating that it was being 'seriously evaded in the neighbourhood through ignorance of the public and the obstinacy of chimney sweeps'. Having told both sweeps and householders exactly what the Act required, they warned that 'inspectors would be appointed to lay information and obtain convictions before the magistrates'. Its warning was not only to sweeps but also to housekeepers who employed boys to sweep their chimneys and was stark but tempered by the hope 'that the exhibition of this notice will be sufficient [for] all who have common feelings of humanity and respect for the laws of the country'.[7] It was not. Sadly, however ingenious the inventions were, none of them did the job as well as climbing boys. What is more, the Hertford machine cost £25, a large capital expense for the average sweep without the backing of a dedicated society of fundraisers such as those in Hitchin and Hertford.

In other parts of the county progress in the use of machines was very slow and magistrates were among the worst offenders, sometimes showing extraordinary ignorance of the law or weakness in applying it. In 1862 a Hemel Hempstead sweep wrote to the Earl of Shaftesbury complaining (wrongly) that he was the only sweep in the county using machines. He told the great reformer that he had taken a case to court against another sweep for sending boys up chimneys, supported by a witness who was a police constable. He claimed that the magistrate had thrown the case out and required him to pay twelve shillings in costs.[8]

Another explanation for the slow adoption of machinery instead of climbing boys was revealed in a letter[9] from a Mary Fairbanks to her friend John Wheeler, a relative of William Tuke, a member of the Hitchin Quaker banking family. The letter is undated but it is clear from its contents that it was written as part of the discussion about the effectiveness of machines. Mary Fairbanks' view was that it was not the efficacy of the machines, the main area of enquiry by the House of Lords Select Committee, but that it required 'men instead of boys to work it. The chimney sweeps protest against it without [meaning 'unless'] they are allowed an advanced [increased] price, so that many are not willing to use it'. She allowed herself to hope that 'if attention is paid in future to new buildings, [and] particularly if our Society [of Friends] will themselves make use of it', progress would be made. Men were more expensive than boys. The price that customers were willing to pay and the need of sweeps to earn a living put pressure on the masters in a competitive market to use cheap climbing boys rather than expensive machines.

Opposition in the House of Lords on other grounds to the abolition of climbing boys came from master sweeps (not from Hertfordshire, none of whom was invited as a witness, but from London, Bristol and other cities with many old mansions), who gave evidence before the Committee of the House of Lords[10] considering the bill that eventually became the 1840 Act for the Regulation of Chimney Sweeps and Chimneys. Climbing boys did two other things besides sweeping away the soot. Two witnesses, Carter and Sanders, objected that machines could not put out chimney fires 'as well as boys [could]'. Robert Taylor, a Bristol master sweep, stated that he very frequently had to send boys up to repair damage to the brickwork, called 'coring'. This required a particular technique, with the boy having to lodge himself with his knees alone, leaving both hands free to do the repairs. The sweep often had to lower materials down from the chimney stacks on the roof.

Not only is there no evidence of climbing boys being taken from workhouses in Hertfordshire, there is evidence to the contrary from the repeated rejection of an attempt by a sweep in Barnet to take a small boy from the workhouse. His attempt was similar to those noted by the Leicestershire magistrates but in Hertfordshire it failed.

Barnet Union of Guardians versus James Furnell in the case of Charles Gwillim[11]

The Guardians of the Poor in the Barnet Union (established as the new union covering parishes in Hertfordshire and Middlesex under the 1834 Poor Law Amendment Act) had quite a protective attitude to boys sought by sweeps as apprentices. James Furnell, a master sweep from Hadley, was given a hard time by the Guardians when he tried to recruit a climbing boy. The master of the workhouse during this case was Benjamin Woodcock and he rejected the request. The decision lay not with Woodcock but with the Guardians. The Barnet Guardians consisted at this time of two vicars, who were chairman and vice-chairman, two farmers, two landowners, a grocer, an innkeeper and an attorney. The request was rejected by them. A few days later Furnell reappeared, saying that he had seen a boy, Charles Gwillim, aged ten and 'just the right size'. Woodcock told him that the Guardians did not approve of boys being apprenticed to sweeps. Undaunted and suggesting rather challengingly that he might seek the Guardians' support to overrule Woodcock, Furnell responded that he knew one of the Guardians, a grocer elected for Chipping Barnet. Either Furnell had seen the boy or the grocer/guardian had chosen Gwillim for him. Visitors were not allowed into workhouses without the permission of a guardian – a rule that Woodcock enforced unflinchingly, seeing off no less a person than Lady Hardwick of Tittenhanger (Lord Hardwick later visited as a member of the legislature). Woodcock then took up the case of Gwillim on his own initiative, interviewing the boy on two separate occasions to enquire whether he wanted to be apprenticed to Furnell. On both occasions the boy said that he did want this. It was an uncharacteristic act by Woodcock, who usually followed the Guardians' guidance on all matters. Under the new Poor Law there was a clear chain of regulation from the Poor Law Commissioners in London through the Guardians to the master. The Barnet Guardians took great care in vetting all applicants for apprenticeships; for example, they refused to approve an application from a London mathematical instrument-maker until they had checked his character.

Some indication of why Gwillim was keen is that the Shenley poor house, where Gwillim lived, was a miserable, neglected place, with frequent floods of water through the decaying roof. It suffered from what would now be called 'planning blight', that is neglect until the new union workhouse in Barnet became available to take its inmates and Shenley could be closed. Two other boys, like Gwillim also natives of Finchley, had absconded.

An insight into why Gwillim might have been keen to become a sweep can be found in the memoirs of Robert Blincoe, as told to his biographer, John Brown.[12] Like Gwillim, Blincoe was a workhouse boy and he startled Brown by recalling how, looking out of his St Pancras Workhouse window, he had seen and envied chimney boys of eight to ten years, tramping the street. All Blincoe saw was the freedom that the boys enjoyed and not how they spent their working hours. Blincoe, like some Hertfordshire workhouse children, was sent north to be apprenticed in cotton mills.

The only explanation for Woodcock's attitude in resisting the Guardians' decision was that he was trying to reduce the poor rate, one of the prime objects of the new

Poor Law, whereas the Barnet Guardians were resisting the requirement of the new Poor Law and showing some compassion. Woodcock was in many ways a compassionate man, being diligent, for example, in rejecting low-grade meat that the local butcher thought good enough for the workhouse inmates. He also acted on the recommendation of the medical officer that some wine, brandy or beer be given as a comfort to elderly inmates (who were often mortally ill). He admitted an injured Scottish drover into the workhouse for treatment, more in the spirit of a medieval monastic hospice than as a place for the incarceration of the idle, undeserving poor.

Furnell, now having the support of the Chipping Barnet grocer/guardian, the master of the workhouse and the boy himself, did not give up his attempt to apprentice Gwillim, despite the steadfastness of the Guardians. In mid-October 1836 Furnell again approached the master and was told by Woodcock, just as forthrightly as before, that he had been 'directed by the Guardians to keep him [Gwillim] as usual'.

Long before the new Poor Law of 1834, Guardians of the Poor had shown a particular resistance to allowing apprenticeships to master sweeps.[13] The Barnet Guardians maintained their pre-1834 consciences in relation to sweeps' apprenticeships whatever the financial demands of the new law.

By the spring of 1837 Furnell decided on a new tack, asking for a girl. This was a hopeless attempt, for the Guardians were even more wary of apprenticing a girl than a boy to a sweep, because of the moral implications. Furnell made an offer (or 'terms' as Woodcock recorded it) to train and lodge her, but not to clothe her. Furnell's offer was less favourable than those laid down by the London Society of Master Sweeps, which required climbing boys or girls to have the facility of a daily wash and a change of clothes once a week, a truckle bed, and one meal a day, compared to the Barnet workhouse inmates' three meals a day with quantities and variety laid down in detail. Furnell was again rejected. By the time of the 1851 census Furnell seems to have left the area. If he remained in Hertfordshire, he had given up his work as a sweep and the failure to engage a small boy to climb chimneys may well have contributed to his failure to build his business as a sweep in the county.

Ways of boosting the sweeps' incomes

Not to have sons as potential climbing boys was very difficult for sweep families. Although there was an increasing demand for the services of sweeps in the county, especially in the first half of the century, their incomes remained low. A steady stream of boys being born was the cheapest way of having a regular supply of climbers. For the Hitchin sweeps, however, the alternative was to marry a plait-maker who could earn more than a sweep. Then, if any girls were born they could follow their mother's trade and the increase in the family income could be considerable. Hitchin sweeps avoided the grinding poverty of Hertford and other sweeps as a result of marriages to plait-makers.

After Hertford, Hitchin was the second most important centre for chimney sweeps. Here the sweeps lived in Hollow Lane, similar to Butcherly Green in Hertford for its squalor. The Howard family were the main sweeps. Its head was Thomas Howard, a former soldier, who had served in Egypt and founded the dynasty. Francis Lucas, of the well-known Quaker family, recalled Howard in his biographical memoirs[14] as 'a kindly man, employing several climbing boys, by whom he was regarded as a kind master.' Chimney-cleaning was done in the early morning after the chimneys from the previous day's fires had cooled. This left the boys free for most of the day, with plenty of time for play, often 'tickling' fish in the River Hiz between the town and Walsworth and in Bury Mead where it is thought that they caught bream and trout.

Lucas, who was an enthusiast for education, does not mention schooling as an element in Howard's kindness but, with the boys having spent the early mornings up a chimney and being covered in soot, school attendance would have been too much to expect of both the boys and the schools.

Lucas said that there were several cases of cancer in the Howard family but Thomas avoided that fate and lived to an old age, for by the 1851 census Howard was recorded as a Chelsea pensioner, still living in Hollow Lane, not far from his family members who carried on the business, and doubtless behaving as a respected patriarch.

William Howard had five daughters and no sons. It is likely that, although himself a master sweep, he worked for another member of the family, having no climbing boys of his own. He was married to a straw-plaiter and all of his daughters followed their mother's trade, so his family would have had a better income than that of most sweeps. James Howard had seventeen-year-old and thirteen-year-old sons who were both sweeps and a younger son who, like most younger sons and daughters in the Howard families, was noted as a 'scholar' in the 1851 census. Jesse Howard was a twenty-one-year-old sweep married to a plaiter. They had had no children by 1851.

Another member of the Howard clan was a widow, Ann, who was recorded as a chimney sweep in the 1851 census, employing four men, all of whom lived in her house. Her elder son, ten-year-old Richard, was a sweep. Her younger son, six-year-old James, was covered by two entries in the 1851 census, one noting him as a 'scholar' and the other as a 'sweep'; the apparent uncertainty about designation suggests prevarication and throws further suspicion on the use of the term 'scholar' for the sons of sweeps. A fifteen-year-old sweep, Joshua Parker, also lived in Ann's house and may be assumed to have been her employee, although he could have been employed by any of the Howard family sweeps in Hollow Lane.

With some income from straw-plaiting it is possible that the younger children in the Howard cases did attend school – either the plait school, where they would have been 'minded', receiving little education, or the fee-paying National School or British School in the town.

The admission registers for the Hitchin Boys' British Schools show that some sons of sweeps attended, but no Howards applied to become scholars there. One sweep's son who did apply was Henry Westley, aged six, of Hollow Lane in 1839. Westley senior's wife was also a plaiter. His seventeen-year-old son was a sweep and two younger sons were 'scholars'. According to the *Hertfordshire Mercury* of 16 August 1851, Westley pleaded guilty to having sent Alfred Izzard, a boy of nine in his employ, up a chimney. He was fined £5. Westley, with sons of climbing boy age, preferred to use other people's sons to do his climbing. Another son of a sweep who was an applicant to the Boys' British School was Henry Williams, also aged six and from Hollow Lane.[15]

Most sweeps increased their incomes by following their London counterparts in collecting night soil. They also sold their soot to farmers, either directly or through soot-dealers, of which there were at least two in Hitchin.

James Garment of the main sweep family in Aldbury near Tring was a seller of soot to farmers. The family lived near the pond at Aldbury and most of their business was in Aldbury and the surrounding villages. James was a commoner of the village and was able to graze his donkey on the common, as well as collect wood for his fire. The latter task would have been given to his son Edwin. Like many sweeps James sold the soot that he collected to local farmers as a fertiliser. Thus the family was not wholly dependent on the income from chimney-sweeping. Edwin became known as 'one of the last climbing boys', according to Ruth, Lady Craufurd[16], a frequent writer on Aldbury. Unlike many of his kind Edwin was not sent entirely naked into the flues but with his toes and knees bound with rags and wearing a hood completely covering his head and shoulders; as it was entirely dark he could not and did not need to see what he was doing whereas the hood reduced the risk of suffocation. His father pushed him up the chimney until the flue became too narrow, when Edwin had to begin climbing. On May Day each year Edwin accompanied his father with the Jack-in-the-Greens, singing and dancing on a tour of the villages, an event mentioned in a folk song, the Marsworth May Song. School log books throughout the county show that attendance declined after storms when branches fell and needed to be collected as firewood. Scavenging in the countryside was typical of the way many sweeps, as well as agricultural labourers and other poor people, survived. Edwin Garment was recorded by Ruth, Lady Craufurd as doing this.

Another way to earn a better living was to combine bricklaying with chimney-sweeping but this was rather a specialist field, with the bricklaying the bigger and better-paid part of the job. The same R. Waller who used the machine sponsored by the Hertford campaigning group was one who combined the two trades. Another was William Willgoss of Batchworth hamlet, Rickmansworth, who lived apart from other Watford sweeps and called himself a 'bricklayer and sweep' in the 1851 census. He had one sweep boy, David Atkins, aged fifteen, working for him. This was not enough labour to run a sweep's business profitably and Atkins was obviously a climber who did repair work supervised by his bricklayer master. The climbing boy's main job in these cases was 'coring', the repair of flue brickwork from the inside, after it had been swept. The general view was that bricklayers could sweep chimneys but not vice versa.

Taking in lodgers was an important source of additional income, as has already been seen with some sweeps and other families in the county. Sarah Perrin of Spicer Street, St Albans, like Mrs Dye (mother of the suffocated James) of Hertford, had been her husband's business partner until his death. By the time of the 1851 census she was a forty-year-old widow who took in lodgers as well as running her sweep's business. She had eight sweeps working for her, including her sixteen-year-old son and seven-year-old nephew, both of whom, like her, had been born in Hitchin. The other members of her team were two boys aged fifteen and eighteen, also born in Hitchin, and the rest were in their early twenties, all unmarried and mostly born in places close to Hitchin or St Albans, although one had been born in Italy. In addition to the eight sweeps, Mrs Perrin had eight lodgers, making a total of seventeen people including herself living in the house. Her situation is an example of the pressures on the poor and how a person of limited education could run two businesses in order to feed her family.

Despite attempts to help the cause of climbing boys and the attempts of the families to lift themselves, including their children, out of abject poverty, the status and condition of the sweep families had improved little by the 1860s.

The slowness of change

Long after the 1840 Act the condition of sweeps and their social ranking had not improved. The *Hertfordshire Mercury* carried an account in August 1859 of a tea meeting held in Hertford Corn Exchange that had the reporter almost swooning at the sight of 400–600 people of all classes ('gentry, clergy, tradespeople and upper working class, as well as those for which the meeting was originally designed') sitting down together and mixing. The origins of the meeting lay in an attempt by the 'Christian ladies' of All Saints Church to get 'the lower classes' to attend the church. The ladies realised that the 'poorest poor', who were the sweeps, had no means of washing in their slum yards, which had no running water, and no clean clothes into which they could change on Sundays. The ladies had collected sufficient clothes for the 'small colony' of sweeps (this was the Butcherly Green area of Hertford, now the location of the bus station). The ladies still managed to persuade only a few to go to All Saints, but more were persuaded to go to the Ragged School in Hertford on Sundays where they were instructed by the town missionary and two of the town's vicars. At the tea itself the sweep families were 'well-behaved', it was reported. Readers were left to assume that the gentry, some of whose ladies preferred to observe from the gallery, and others were also well-behaved. This gushing report demonstrated not only the continuance of the sweep families' position at the bottom of the social system but also showed that their working conditions had improved little despite the 1840 Act, which had banned the use of climbing boys below the age of twenty and thus in effect banned it totally. Like previous legislation, this Act had quickly fallen into disuse and by 1859 little had changed in Hertford because economics and social status were the determinant factors, not legislation. There was little improvement until the last quarter of the century.

In 1875 Shaftesbury's Act put an end to the remaining evils of climbing boys who, already much reduced in number, were finally grounded, their role at last taken over by machines and the owners of the grand houses finally forced to refashion their flues to accommodate them. Goldings, the site of James Dye's suffocation, was demolished and rebuilt in the 1860s. It is not known whether the difficulty of reconstructing the system of chimneys and flues was insuperable and therefore played a part in the decision to do this.

In Hertford the last quarter of the century saw continuous improvement of building standards, better sanitation and the provision of clean water supplies in most places but not in Butcherly Green.[17] The Hollow Lane and St Andrews Street slums in Hitchin were not pulled down until the 1920s.

The Butcherly Green slums remained a place of violence until the end. There was no love lost between some of the Butcherly Green sweep families. In 1875 the Bland and Baker families, descendants of the Blands and Bakers who were involved in the court cases of 1847 and 1851, were in court together. Walter Bland was found guilty of having assaulted John William Baker, both still of Butcherly Green. The *Hertfordshire Mercury* of 11 December 1875 reported that Bland was sentenced to two months' hard labour. It was said that 'he had been in trouble ever since he was eight years of age'.

Endnotes

1. *Report to the general board of health on Hertford*, 1850.
2. J. Cooper, *Hertford: a history* (Chichester, 2007), p. 101.
3. Obituary of Minto Farquhar, 1866, Obituary file, HALS.
4. F.M. Page, *History of Hertford*, 2nd edn (Hertford, 1993), pp. 182–3.

5. BPP 1833 (450) XX.1, paragraph 63.
6. Lawson Thompson scrapbook, HM, vol. 1B, pp. 192–3.
7. *Ibid.*, p. 192.
8. B. Cullingford, *British chimney sweeps* (Sussex, 2000), p. 179.
9. MS letter from Mary Fairbanks to John Wheeler, HALS, D/ESE/C1.
10. BPP, *Minutes of evidence taken before the Select Committee of the House of Lords to consider the Bill entitled an Act for the Regulation of Chimney Sweeps and Report to the House*, paragraphs 10–23, July 1840.
11. The diary of Benjamin Woodcock, master of the Barnet workhouse and the minutes of the Barnet guardians, HALS, 70876 and BG/BAR/1. Furnell's name is spelled in different ways throughout Woodcock's MS diary and transcribers do not agree on the most appropriate spelling. I have used 'Furnell' throughout for consistency.
12. J. Waller, *The real Oliver Twist* (Thriplow, 2005), p. 53.
13. BPP 1843 (430) XIII.307, *Children's employment commission*, paragraph 623.
14. *Hitchin biography*, copied from the manuscript of Francis Lucas of Hitchin with additions by C. Loftus Barnham, 1892, HM, p. 357.
15. Hitchin boys' British school index of admissions.
16. Ruth, Lady Craufurd, *Hertfordshire Countryside*, 20/150 (October 1972), pp. 26–7.
17. Cooper, *Hertford*, pp. 118–19.

Chapter 8

Conclusion

The nineteenth century was a period of great, and in some cases very rapid, change. So it was for the children of the labouring poor. In the first half of the century many children were in work from a very early age for very long hours, as young as three or four in the case of straw-plaiting, and certainly from the age of seven or eight in many other occupations. At first there was no protection at all for the young workers.

Legislation to protect them and to limit their hours was very slow in coming and took until the 1860s and 1870s to spread to almost every sphere of work; the Workshops Act of 1867 brought most trades under regulation while the Factory and Workshop Act of 1878 encompassed the rest and laid the foundations of modern factory legislation. Accidents at work were a problem throughout the century and it was not until the 1890s, after pressure from, among others, the factory inspectorate, that adequate legislation was introduced to bring in rules concerning safety and the regulation of the workplace environment. Even so, there was still a high rate of accidents at work at the turn of the century and young workers from the age of eleven in Hertfordshire in occupations like agriculture were still vulnerable.

The interviews that factory inspectors conducted with labouring children from the 1830s to the 1870s give a graphic picture of working conditions and some of the attitudes of the young workers at the time. It seems that they accepted their lot stoically, having known no other. Those working in the factories were grateful for small mercies like being allowed to warm themselves in front of a fire when they got bitterly cold, to sleep for a few hours when they were on twenty-four-hour shifts, to dry out their trousers when they got them wet in the course of their work and, in some cases, not to be beaten by their employers. They accepted that they should contribute to the family finances in some way and in some cases were proud to do so. Those who suffered the most, with very few mitigating circumstances, were the children employed in some brickfields and those who worked as climbing boys for chimney sweeps. The masters treated them very harshly and unfeelingly until forced by effective legislation in 1871 and 1875 respectively to stop employing young children altogether. Brickmaking in Hertfordshire was declining at that time anyway because vast fields of more easily exploited clay were discovered in neighbouring counties, especially Bedfordshire, and brickmaking began to be mechanised. The owners of mansions with complicated flues had to rebuild or reconstruct so that rodded brushes or machines could be used.

Other occupations which had virtually disappeared by the end of the century were straw-plaiting, destroyed by the import of cheap Chinese plait, and silk-throwing, also threatened by foreign competition, which resulted in only two silk mills remaining in the county in 1900. One growth area was domestic service where more young people were employed because middle-class families were able to afford to employ servants and to enjoy the social status this brought. Indeed the social hierarchy was, if anything, more rigid at the end of the century and it was not until the upheavals of the First World War, involving most adults and many boys who were not quite adults, that changes came.

Changes in education as well as factory legislation had a profound effect on the lives of poor children. The early factory inspectors' reports highlighted the patchy nature of schooling. Some children received no education or went to plaiting schools where they had little education. Others attended a variety of schools such as Sunday schools, dame schools, National or British Schools or schools set up by their employers. Many did not attend consistently and only gained the ability to read, and sometimes to write, but little else. By 1900 all children were supposed to be in school. Full-time attendance until at least the age of eleven had been compulsory since 1880 and schooling free since 1891. That did not mean that all children had an uninterrupted education as many Hertfordshire children were taken out of school, even in the 1890s, to help on the land when farmers needed extra labour, as many school log books show.

The diet of many children probably improved as a result of cheap food imports but the families of agricultural labourers remained poor as wages hardly improved and the money that the children under eleven years of age had earned was lost when they attended school. Some, as at Tewin, did keep their children away from school for a few days in term time to earn a little money because 'we are very poor and sadly need it'. If families became so poor that they had to turn to the Board of Guardians, at least outdoor relief had been reinstated and they might be able to stay out of the workhouses. If they had to enter the workhouse they would find that conditions within were not as grim as they had been earlier in the century.

One area where there was little improvement by 1900 was that of housing and amenities such as a good water supply, proper sanitation and waste disposal. There were numerous attempts to improve amenities in places such as Watford where various local government committees tried to tackle deep-seated problems. Sometimes there was actual hindrance as when, in 1851, the Marquess of Salisbury used his influence in the House of Lords to block the setting-up of a local board of health for Hertford. It was not until the 1920s and 1930s that the slum areas of many towns were cleared and better housing provided. Changes came even more slowly in the villages and some had to wait until after the Second World War to have a reliable water supply and proper sanitation.

The death rate for young children was still very high in 1900, about one in eight children dying before they were five. Things did not improve in Hertfordshire until the effects were felt of the pioneering work done by the newly appointed health visitors with mothers and babies at the beginning of the next century. During the nineteenth century vaccination had reduced the incidence of smallpox, and cholera had not reappeared for many years, but there were plenty of other diseases to which children could succumb such as typhoid, measles, scarlet fever and diphtheria. Again it was not until the twentieth century that poorer people got some access to affordable medical services. School medical services were not introduced throughout the country until 1906.

However, in spite of the lack of progress in some children's lives, when one looks at the working lives of children in 1800 and 1900 it can be said that there had been improvements and there were more to come in the first years of the twentieth century.

Bibliography

Primary sources

In manuscript

Documents held at Hertfordshire Archives and Local Studies (hereafter HALS)

School log books, in particular those of:

Anstey School, HEd1/1

Boxmoor School, HEd1/210

Chorleywood School HEd1/193

Flaunden School, HEd1/111

High Wych School HEd1/100

Norton School, HEd1/44

Pirton School, HEd1/83

St Albans Abbey School, HEd1/198

St Ippollyts School Off Acc 1027

St Mary's School, Hitchin, HEd2/7

St Mary's School, Ware, D/P116

Walsworth School, D/P/53

Wareside School, HEd1/113

Potten End log books are still held at the school.

Most of the records of the British Schools, Hitchin are at the British Schools Museum, Hitchin though a few documents relating to the early history of the British girls' school Hitchin, including annual reports from the 1820s and 30s, are held at HALS, 67528-31.

Records of Poor Law Unions and their school attendance and rural sanitary committees:

Barnet Union BG/BAR including the diary, 1836–9, of Benjamin Woodcock, Master of Barnet workhouse, 70876

Berkhamsted Union, BG/BERK

Bishop's Stortford Union, BG/BIS

Buntingford Union, BG/BUN

Hertford Union, BG/HER

Hitchin Union, BG/HIT

Royston Union, BG/ROY
Ware Union, BG/WAR

MS letter from Mary Fairbanks to John Wheeler, D/ESE/C1

Documents held at Hitchin Library
Lawrence, E.L., *Diary of a village* (*Codicote*), ref H45 376 660 9

Documents held at Hitchin Museum
Lawson Thompson scrapbooks
Diary of Francis Lucas in manuscript
Hertfordshire Express newspaper, various dates with a nearly complete run from 1890 to 1900

Documents held at the Centre for Buckinghamshire Studies, Aylesbury
Aylesbury board of guardians minute book, 1838–9, G/2/3

Documents held at the National Archives
Correspondence between the Poor Law commissioners and individual unions, MH12
Bishops Stortford, 4536
Royston, 4639

Documents held at the City of Westminster archives
Minutes of the overseers of the poor and boards of guardians of the following parishes:
St George's, Hanover Square
St James's, Piccadilly
St Margaret's, Westminster
St Martin-in-the-Fields

In print

Parliamentary Debates (Hansard) Commons and Lords throughout the century, in particular those that include speeches about child labour in Hertfordshire and those that cover debates about legislation thereon

British Parliamentary Papers:
1818 (136) IV.1, *Report from the select committee on the education of the lower orders*
1833 (450) XX.1, *Royal commission on the employment of children in factories*
1834 (572) IX.1, *Report from Select Committee on the State of Education*
1835 (62) XLI.1–XLIII.1, *Abstract of answers and returns relative to the state of education in England and Wales*
1843 (430) XIII.307, *Children's employment commission*
1843 (431) XIV.1, *Children's employment commission*
1861 (2895) LXII.397, *Miscellaneous statistics of the United Kingdom, part III*
1864 (3416) XXVIII.1, *Sixth report of the medical officer of the Privy Council*

1864 (3414) XXII.1, *Children's employment commission (1862)*
1866 (3678) XXIV.1, *Children's employment commission (1862)*
1867–8 (4068) XVII.1, *Commission on the employment of children, young persons and women in agriculture (1867)*
1868–9 (4202) XIII.1, *Commission on the employment of children, young persons and women in agriculture (1867)*
1873 (c.745) XIX.41, *Reports of inspectors of factories to Secretary of State for Home Department, May–October 1872*

Reports to the general board of health on the towns of Great Amwell and Ware, Hertford, Hitchin, Hoddesdon, Hemel Hempstead and Watford, 1849–53. HALS

Censuses of 1841, 1851, 1861, 1871 and 1891, including the analyses by age and occupations published after each census. The 1851 census has been transcribed and put on disk by the University of Hertfordshire.

Childs, R.J., *Testimony and portraits of men and women living in Hertfordshire, who suffered by protection in the good old days* (Watford, 1906), HALS photocopy in pamphlet file 1 on agriculture

County Chronicle, 1816, 1818–26, 1827–32 on microfilm at HALS.

Hertfordshire Mercury, 1825–30, 1844–87, 1888–1937 on microfilm at HALS.

Obituary file compiled from local papers held at HALS.

Osborne's London and Birmingham railway guide, 1840, HALS

Theses

Jennings, S.A., 'A ravelled skein: the silk industry in south-west Hertfordshire, 1790–1890', PhD thesis (University of Hertfordshire, 2002)
Wheatly, C., 'The pauper girls at Tring silk mill between 1840 and 1871', course DA301 (Open University, 2000)

Secondary sources

Agar, N.E., *Hitchin's straw plait industry* (Hitchin, 1998)
Agar, N.E., *Behind the plough: agrarian society in nineteenth-century Hertfordshire* (Hatfield, 2005)
Allen, S. (ed.), *W. Branch Johnson's articles on Hertfordshire history* (Codicote, undated)
Austin, W., *Tring silk mill* (Tring, 2008)
Bagley, J.J. and Bagley, A.J.G., *The state of education in England and Wales, 1833–1968* (London, 1968)
Beachcroft, T.O. and Emms, W.B., *Five hide village: a history of Datchworth in Hertfordshire* (Datchworth, 1984)
Bennet, R., *Hertford street and place names* (Hertford, 1996)
Bennett, A., *A working life: child labour through the nineteenth century*, 2nd edn (Launceston, 1995)

Boyson, R., *The Ashworth cotton enterprise* (Oxford, 1970)
Branch Johnson, W., *Industrial archaeology of Hertfordshire* (Newton Abbot, 1970)
Brown, J., *The English market town* (Marlborough, 1986)
Bryant, V.J.M., *A history of Potten End* (Cheshunt, 1986)
Bryant, G. and Baker, G., (eds) *W. Lucas, a Quaker journal, 1804–61*, two volumes (London, 1934)
Buckingham, J., *A window on Victorian St Albans* (St Albans, 1988)
Burnett, J., *Useful toil, autobiographies of working people from the 1820s to the 1920s* (London, 1984)
Bush, S., *The silk industry* (Oxford, 2009)
Cooper, A., *A harvest of Hexton* (Hexton, 1986)
Cooper, J., *Hertford: a history* (Chichester, 2007)
Coutts Smith, J. (compiler), *A Hertfordshire sampler* (Hertford, 1980)
Crooks, E., *The factory inspectors: a legacy of the industrial revolution* (Stroud, 2005)
Crosby, T., Douglas, P., Fletcher S., Gimson, M., Howlett, B., Humphries, P. and Walker, S., *Jeeves Yard: a dynasty of Hitchin builders and brickmakers* (Baldock, 2003)
Cullingford, B., *British chimney sweeps* (Sussex, 2000)
Cullingford, B., *Chimneys and chimney sweeps* (Princes Risborough, 2003)
Cunningham, H., *The invention of childhood* (London, 2006)
Cussans, J., *History of Hertfordshire*, three volumes (Hertford, 1880)
Davis, J., *Straw plait* (Aylesbury, 1981)
Davis, J., *Aldbury: the open village* (Aldbury, 1987)
Deacon, A. and Walne, P.J.E., *A professional Hertfordshire tramp, J.E. Cussans* (Hertford, 1987)
Dodwell, F., *Hitchin British schools, schooldays 1810–1900* (Letchworth Garden City, 1993)
Dony, J.G., *A history of the straw hat industry* (Luton, 1942)
Dunk, G., *Around St Albans with Geoff Dunk* (St Albans, 1985)
Evans, G.E., *Ask the fellows who cut the hay* (London, 1944)
Evans, G.E., *The crooked scythe* (London, 1993)
Evans, J., *The endless web* (London, 1955)
Farris, N., *The Wymondleys* (Hertford, 1989)
Festing, S., *The story of lavender* (Sutton, 1982)
Fleck, A., *Hitchin in old photographs* (Stroud, 1994)
Fogg, H. (ed.), *Waterford in times past* (Waterford, undated)
Foster, A., *Market town: Hitchin in the nineteenth century*, ed. L. Munby (Hitchin, 1987)
Francatelli, C.E.M., *A plain cookery book for the working classes* (originally published London, 1861, reprinted Whitstable, 1998)
Gear, G. (ed.), *The diary of Benjamin Woodcock, master of the Barnet union workhouse, 1836–8* (Hertford, 2010)
Grey, E., *Cottage life in a Hertfordshire village: how the agricultural labourers lived and fared in the late 1860s and 70s* (originally published St Albans, 1934, reprinted Harpenden, 1977)
Griffin, K., *Transported beyond the seas* (Welwyn Garden City, 1997)
Grof, L., *Children of straw* (Buckingham, 1988)
Goodman, A., *The story of the Abbey School: a nineteenth-century national school* (St Albans, 1991)
Goose, N., *Population, economy and family structure in Hertfordshire in 1851, vol. 1 the Berkhamsted region* (Hatfield, 1996)

Goose, N., *Population, economy and family structure in Hertfordshire in 1851, vol. 2, St Albans and its region* (Hatfield, 2000)
Goose, N., 'The straw plait and hat trades in nineteenth-century Hertfordshire', in N. Goose (ed.), *Women's work in industrial England* (Hatfield, 2007)
Goose, N., 'Child employment prospects in nineteenth-century Hertfordshire in perspective: varieties of childhood?', unpublished article
Gutchen, R.M. et al., *Down and out in Hertfordshire* (Hatfield, 1984)
Hammond, M., *Bricks and brickmaking* (Oxford, 2009)
Horn, P., *The Victorian country child* (Kineton, 1974)
Horn, P., *Life in a Victorian household* (Stroud, 2007)
Horner, L., *On the employment of children: in factories and other works in the United Kingdom and in some foreign countries* (London, 1840)
James, S. (ed.), *Two hundred years of Tewin school* (Tewin, 1992)
Kingsford, P., *North Mymms people in Victorian times* (Hatfield, 1984)
Kingsford, P., *North Mymms schools and their children, 1700–1964* (originally published Hatfield, 1987, reprinted 1999)
Knight, J. and Flood, S., *Two nineteenth-century diaries* (Hertford, 2002)
Langland, A., Ginn, P. and Goodman, R., *Victorian farm: rediscovering forgotten skills* (London, 2008)
Lucas, J., *Phebe's Hitchin book* (Hitchin, 2009)
Luck, L., 'A little of my life', *London Mercury*, 13 (1925–6)
Massey, G., *My lyrical life, poems old and new* (London, 1889)
Mingay, G.E., *Rural life in Victorian England* (London, 1979)
Munby, L., *The Hertfordshire landscape* (London, 1977)
Page, F.M., *History of Hertford*, 2nd edn (Hertford, 1993)
Perrins, L., 'Recalling Hertfordshire's brickworks', *Hertfordshire Countryside*, 36 (April 1981)
Perrins, L., 'Hertfordshire brickworks: a gazetteer', *Hertfordshire Archaeology and History*, 14 (2004–05)
Possee, P., *The weaver and the throwster: the nineteenth-century silk industry of Essex and Suffolk* (Braintree, 2006)
Purkis, J., *The courts and yards of Hertford* (Hertford, 1982)
Rance, D., *St Ippolyts* (Baldock, 1987)
Rook, T., 'Welwyn viaduct', *The Welwyn Times*, 28 July (1959)
Shorter, A.H., *Paper making in the British Isles* (Newton Abbot, 1971)
Slater, T. and Goose, N., *A county of small towns: the development of Hertfordshire's urban landscape to 1800* (Hatfield, 2008)
Smith, G., *Our canal population* (Coalville, 1875)
Smith, G., *Cry of the children from the brickyards of England* (Coalville, 1880)
Stebbing, E.E., *Echoes from Shenley's past* (Shenley, 1988)
Waller, J., *The real Oliver Twist* (Thriplow, 2005)
Watford Museum, *The high street revisited* (Watford, 1991)
Wayne, J., (ed.) *A foot on three daisies* (Pirton, 1987)
Wayne, J., *Morning has broken, the story of Pirton school* (Pirton, 1987)
Young, A., *General view of the agriculture of Hertfordshire* (originally published 1804, reprinted Newton Abbot, 1971)

Index

Page numbers in italics refer to illustrations.